ISSUES IN FOCUS

Gaining a Clear Biblical Perspective
on the Complex Issues of Our Time

Compiled by
Margaret Rosenberger

Rega

A Division
Ventura, C

D1166487

Published by Regal Books
A Division of Gospel Light
Ventura, California, U.S.A.
Printed in U.S.A.

Scripture quotations in this publication are taken from:

The HOLY BIBLE, NEW INTERNATIONAL VERSION. Copyright © 1973, 1978, 1984 International Bible Society. Used by permission of Zondervan Bible Publishers.
RSV—Revised Standard Version. From *RSV* of the Bible, copyrighted 1946 and 1952 by the Division of Christian Education of the NCCC in the U.S.A., and used by permission.
KJV—The Authorized King James Version.
NASB—New American Standard Bible. © The Lockman Foundation 1960, 1962, 1963, 1968, 1971, 1973, 1975. Used by permission.

Some of the sessions in *Issues in Focus* are revisions of two earlier courses titled, *Hot Buttons* and *Hot Buttons II.*

Library of Congress Cataloging-in-Publication Data

Issues in focus / compiled by Margaret Rosenberger.
    p.   cm.
    Bibliography: p.
    ISBN 0-8307-1332-8
    1. Christian ethics. 2. Ethics in the Bible. 3. Social ethics. 4. Social values. 5. United States—Moral conditions.
    I. Rosenberger, Margaret.
BJ1275.I84   1989   89-31025
261—dc19   CIP

5 6 7 8 9 10 11 12 13 14 15 16 17 18 19 20 21 22 / 00 99 98 97 96 95

Rights for publishing this book in other languages are contracted by Gospel Literature International (GLINT). GLINT also provides technical help for the adaptation, translation, and publishing of Bible study resources and books in scores of languages worldwide. For further information, contact GLINT, Post Office Box 4060, Ontario, California, 91761-1003, U.S.A., or the publisher.

Contents

1

Who's in Control?

JIM REEVES

One of the gravest situations facing our society is the use and abuse of intoxicants, a category which includes drugs and alcohol. The material in this chapter is designed to provide factual information about these substances along with biblical guidelines regarding their use.

WHAT DRUGS ARE AND WHAT THEY DO

What is a drug? It has been called a powerful substance that can change one's mood, perception or way of thinking. Alcohol does this and so does cocaine, but what about soda pop? Can it change one's mood or feelings? Can it change one's perception or senses? Or can it change one's ability to think clearly? Most soda pop contains caffeine, a stimulant drug served in a mild dose, and sugar. Is sugar a drug? It strongly affects the body, and experts say it affects mental function and creates hyperactivity. How about chocolate? It contains sugar, along with a natural chemical substance related to caffeine. We could go on with the list. What then is a drug? Is it heroin, cocaine, marijuana and alcohol only? Should we include coffee, colas and candy? According to our definition a drug can be almost any substance, and these substances cannot always be avoided. Without a doubt, we use drugs of all kinds on a daily basis. Chemical substances like caffeine in colas and coca in chocolate are in such small doses they seem to harm no one. Over-the-counter medications for colds and congestion contain small amounts of mood and mind altering drugs, but with precautions they are OK for most people to use. Doctor's prescriptions are stronger over-the-counter medications, but we count on the physician's judgment not to over-medicate us. Street drugs are frightening because everyone in authority says they are dangerous to use. We need to know what these chemicals can do to our bodies.

Alcohol and Other Sedatives

Alcohol is the most popular intoxicant in the world, consumed by millions of people on a daily basis. Alcoholic beverages have been known for thousands of years. Noah discovered their affects and got drunk not long after leaving the ark (see Gen. 9:20,21). Old Testament writers and ancient historians have recorded testimonies of the good and ill effects of drinking. Alcohol is known for its sedative effect. In small doses it can: help reduce stress in the body; promote health and digestion (see 1 Tim. 5:23); decrease heart attack risks (ask your doctor); and help in the relief of pain (see Prov. 31:6,7). In large doses over a period of time, alcohol has been observed to produce drunkenness and the destruction of cells in vital organs of our body. And it is addictive. You may have heard all about the destructive effects of alcoholism on relationships and on the body.

Alcohol is an interesting intoxicant to study since it is used by so many people. Experts in the field of chemical substances call alcohol a sedative or depressant. At first glance alcohol does not seem like a sedative. In low doses it makes people feel relaxed, happy, cheerful and very lively. At this point the alcohol has lowered the person's sensitivity to outside stimulation. A person feels less inhibited or restrained from behaving according to the way he or she feels inside. Watch some people you know who drink a little and see if they allow themselves to be happy or playful. The more one drinks the more relaxed one feels. At some point one gets drunk. Drunkenness robs the person of the ability to speak clearly and to walk with steady legs. Continued drinking eventually leads to a complete loss of consciousness.

Aside from alcohol, there are other chemicals that act as sedatives in the body. Doctors use tranquilizers, anesthetics and pain relievers to help their patients feel less pain and cope with their illnesses. The effects of drugs like Valium, Librium and other "downers" are similar to those of alcohol. Doctors also use narcotics to help sedate people, but these substances have a far more powerful effect on the body.

Narcotics

A narcotic dulls the senses and causes a person to sleep. Narcotics cause sedative effects similar to those of the drugs in the previous category. Narcotics do more than sedate the nervous system (like depressants), they sedate the sensors in the brain, thus creating a high sense of euphoria. Narcotic drugs like Percodan, Percoset, Darvoset and morphine are used by physicians to help their patients feel less pain while the body is healing. Opium is the parent plant of all narcotic drugs. We may suspect that the gall which was added to wine during the time of Christ was a narcotic drug because of its potential to relieve the pain experienced on the cross (see Matt. 27:34). Even though narcotics are effective with pain, they are also highly addictive. Doctors prescribe them with caution and try to keep their patients from becoming dependent on them. Unfortunately many do. On the street, narcotic drugs like opium, heroin, codeine and morphine are potent chemicals that leave a person open to dependency. Medical authorities suggest following these rules with narcotic drugs:

1. Use them only for severe physical pain or discomfort.
2. Never inject a narcotic into the body for nonmedical purposes. Such usage can leave you open to repeated experiences and can lead to dependency on the substance.
3. Even when a narcotic provides extreme pleasure the first time, there is no guarantee you will experience a repeat performance a second time. Addiction can happen when a person continues to pursue that elusive pleasure.

Stimulants

Doctors also use drugs that elevate a person's mood. Many people use stimulants every day. You may have seen a TV commercial picturing a scene much like a police chase. Two guys in a car chase a motorcyclist through the city. The passenger in the car is obviously nervous and worried as his partner goes through hairpin turns and several near-misses. The punch line to the commercial is "Life is stimulating enough for some people, so for them we have made caffeine free (_____) cola." Obviously this cola company knew the stimulating effect that caffeine has on the body's system. Stimulants of all kinds activate, energize and make a person more alert. Caffeine in colas or coffee is compared to small doses of prescription medication or street drugs. Doctors prescribe anti-depressant drugs to stimulate the body's system. Stimulants are found in cold medications to offset the drowsiness experienced from its use. Speed, crank, uppers are just a few of the slang words used on the street to describe stimulants.

The most controversial drug in the category of stimulants is cocaine—also known as coke—which is a derivative of the leaves of the coca plant.

Today cocaine abuse is the fastest growing drug problem in America for both adults and school-age children.[1] It is available in a new form called "crack" or "rock" and sold at low prices. Crack is actually a variation of freebasing, which converts sniffable cocaine crystals into a base form of cocaine that is smokable. The high received from crack is far more intense than that which is received from snorted cocaine. It also works faster and is more euphoric. Arnold Washton, a psychopharmacologist at Fair Oaks Hospital in Summit, New Jersey, states that crack is the most addictive drug known to man right now.[2]

Whether snorted, injected or smoked, cocaine can prove fatal. Frightening and unpredictable, it can kill habitual users as well as first-time users. Heroes from both the entertainment and athletic worlds have been among its victims. Although death can come in numerous ways, it usually comes quickly. Causes include lung failure, violent brain seizures, heart attacks, arrhythmias and strokes. Dr. Washton states that the real danger from crack is that the drug comes to control your life by changing your brain chemistry.[3]

Psychedelics

LSD, Mescaline, Magic Mushrooms and MDA are some names of the groups of chemicals called psychedelics or hallucinogens. They are not prescribed by doctors but are found only on the street. Some users of these drugs claim they can explore the mind and probe the origins of religious feelings. Nonusers are fearful of these drugs because they consider them dangerous chemicals capable of driving people to insanity or suicide. As powerful as these substances are, one's state of mind and mood contribute a great deal to the outcome of one's "trip" or drug experience. Visions and hallucinations come from within, and these drugs unleash whatever lies deep in the mind. This is not to say that you should use these drugs on the basis of these descriptions. Psychedelics are powerful chemicals that can cause great emotional trauma and some physical ill effects. They also cause flashbacks at a later time with unpredictable results.

Marijuana

The final chemical for this discussion is marijuana. Marijuana has been used since ancient times. It's abuse dates back as long as that of alcohol. The product of the hemp plant, Cannabis sativa, which provides fiber used in making rope, it is an edible plant, an oil, and a medicine. The intoxicating part comes from the sticky resin exuded by the female plant. Historians through the centuries have described several instances where Assyrians and Persians used hemp-type plants for intoxicating purposes.

Marijuana, also known as pot, grass, "jah" and weed, has a unique characteristic. It can act like a sedative and a stimulant almost at the same time. It can be abused more easily than psychedelics can because it can be used more frequently and continuously through a variety of different activities in one day. Since it has the ability to heighten one's perceived enjoyment in activities, it tends to encourage continued use. People sometimes suggest that smoking pot leads to heroin or LSD usage. Although marijuana has no chemical effect that could push a person to use these "harder" drugs, using marijuana can introduce a person to the experience of using drugs and can make the use of drugs seem more familiar and comfortable. Although most authorities feel that it is not physically addicting, it may lead to psychological dependence.

Scientific studies show that frequent marijuana use may: damage the lungs; affect sex hormone levels (especially for adolescents); and strain the heart.[4] The main danger of smoking marijuana is that it will get away from you. Continued use will develop a habit of usage that will be hard to break. Every activity can become associated with smoking marijuana so that you no longer control your smoking but your smoking controls you.

HOW TO RELATE TO DRUGS

We have spent a lot of time looking at what various drugs do to our bodies. You may be asking yourself, "What drugs are permissible for me to use? When is it OK to use them? Does God say anything about using drugs of any kind?" The Bible does give some guidelines for the use of intoxicants. We will consider these in four major categories: social customs; ignorance and curiosity; avoiding problems; and medical purposes.

Social Customs: All of us come from various social and cultural backgrounds. You may have friends who drink wine as part of their meals. To them it is a family tradition to drink on social occasions. Other families will not touch any kind of drink; some condemn anyone who does. Family traditions are a part of what makes us all different. But we need to put our family traditions aside long enough to look at some passages from the Bible.

The Bible does not give a blanket rule forbidding drinking. It does say that we are not to get drunk nor associate with drunks. Paul tells us in Ephesians 5:18 that we are not to, "get drunk on wine, which leads to debauchery." He is here warning against the sin of drunkenness, a sin common among the pagans (see 1 Pet. 4:3,4). Drinking to excess at their festivals, they would sing obscene and profane songs to Bacchus, the god of wine. And as drunkenness does not stand alone, they would become inflamed by inordinate lusts and gross sensuality. When drinking too much leads to other sins and to poor and foolish choices, then obviously a person is harming himself or herself and others. In addition, the same verse from 1 Peter tells us to be controlled by the Holy Spirit. Those who choose to drink need to ask, "Who's in control, Alcohol or God?" And they need to remember that

Christians' bodies are God's temple, bought at the price of Jesus' death (see 1 Cor. 6:19,20).

Too much wine or beer leaves an individual in a position to make poor choices and can lead one astray (see Prov. 20:1). Paul points out in Galatians 5:21 that drunkenness is an act of the sinful nature of which Christians are not to be a part. In Romans 13:13 Paul portrays drunkenness as an act of sin and darkness. Getting drunk is not wise.

The Bible even hits hard on associating with drunkards. Some fatherly advice comes from Proverbs 23:20,21, which says not to associate with drunkards or gluttons. The association may lead to drinking, but the picture points out that this kind of group goes nowhere. Peter shows us in 1 Peter 4:3,4 that drunkenness is indeed associated with the old nature and other worldly practices of the past. "Put away the past" is Peter's point, "including your associates and friends who get drunk." Paul goes even farther to say that any professing Christian who drinks heavily is not to be associated with by other Christians (see 1 Cor. 5:11). "A drunkard who says he is a Christian should not be allowed to eat at your dinner table," is another way Paul could have said it. What a statement!

What about drinking to be sociable? Did not Jesus turn water into wine at the wedding in Cana? (see John 2:1-10. Many Christians believe that the wine was non-alcoholic). As mentioned earlier, drinking is not condemned in the Bible, drunkenness is. A good example of drinking is Jesus' visit to the wedding in Cana (see John 2:1-11). Everyone present at the wedding was there to socialize and celebrate the good favor that had come to the bridegroom. The environment was just right for everyone to have a good time, but social customs most likely prevented overuse.

Not long after Jesus arrived, they ran out of wine. If wine was wrong for the party He would not have created more. His decision to create wine for the party apparently showed His acceptance of the use of a potential intoxicant for a socially acceptable celebration.

Paul wrote, "So whether you eat or drink or whatever you do, do it all for the glory of God. Do not cause anyone to stumble, whether Jews, Greeks or the church of God" (1 Cor. 10:31,32).

The other side of the sociability coin, however, is our obligation to other people. Paul wrote, "So whether you eat or drink or whatever you do, do it all for the glory of God. Do not cause anyone to stumble, whether Jews, Greeks or the church of God" (1 Cor. 10:31,32). One Christian may be able to use a moderate amount of wine with no problem. But if another Christian, seeing the first one use wine, decides to try it and gets drunk or strays away from God, the first Christian has caused the second to stumble. Similarly, if a Christian is trying to win a friend to Christ, and the friend feels that Christians should not drink, then the Christian friend should avoid drinking in order not to put up a barrier to the other's conversion.

Ignorance and Curiosity
Maybe you or someone you know has experienced a situation similar to the one that follows: John, a new believer, attends a major league ballgame with four co-workers. Jerry pulls a joint (a marijuana cigarette) out of his pocket and lights up. He offers to share the joint with the guys. John was not aware of the fact that Jerry smoked pot. It looks interesting enough, and all the guys want to smoke it. John thinks for a moment about his family and the warnings he received from his parents and school authorities when he was a teenager to stay away from any form of drugs. But John decides to try it along with his friends. He

feels some apprehension and is a little nervous. "Wow! What a feeling!" he thinks to himself. He feels good and relaxed after a few hits, and at the same time he is experiencing some anxiety, even paranoia. Everyone is enjoying the exhilarating feelings. Once in a while one of the guys looks over his shoulder to be sure other fans have not noticed and informed the park authorities.

Suddenly several security officers step out of a nearby tunnel. Immediately the joint is put out. The officers walk down the aisle past John and his friends. John feels like his heart has stopped and he breaks out in a cold sweat. Every noise and sound seems heightened and fear overtakes him. What caused the intense fear in John? How could John have avoided this experience?

As the story pointed out, ignorance of what a drug can and will do to one's system is not wise. A serious problem when using anything in ignorance is panic. You may know someone who was slipped a drug without his or her knowledge. The unsuspecting person may have experienced panic, anxiety, fear and personal doubt of his or her sanity during the experience. Taking a substance you suspect is a drug just because your friends find it acceptable can produce fear, anxiety and paranoia. These reactions may be realized because you don't know what to expect and you may have some fear of getting arrested. "Bad trips" on a hallucinogenic or narcotic can be caused by a panic reaction to the drug.

Ignorance of aftereffects can cause problems as well. Having a good experience turn bad (crashing) can produce depression and an extreme desire to get back to the high. Depression is a common reaction to loss of a good experience. If someone does not realize this fact, they may associate the depression with some other problem and they may use drugs to avoid the emotional pain.

Our curiosity urges us to find out about things in life. Experience is often the best teacher—but not in the area of drugs. Read what you can about all kinds of drugs, and learn what you can from others who know. Remember, using anything out of ignorance can be dangerous.

Avoiding Problems

People use drugs for various reasons. Staff people in drugs and alcohol rehabilitation centers find most of those reasons are to avoid problems or trying situations in life. Some areas are: avoiding conflicts with friends or family members; avoiding feelings of pain over loss of a relationship; destroying oneself because of a poor self-image; "consumable courage" just to function on a day-to-day basis. These are extreme examples of course, but these cases don't just happen. They are worked up to, built from small seeds of guilt, doubt, hurt, anger, fear, loneliness, boredom and so on. These seeds can grow to full problems when left unresolved.

For a Christian to use a chemical substance in order to avoid problems means he or she is giving up letting God control the problem.

When people decide to use a substance to avoid facing problems in life, then they are allowing that substance to be in charge of their lives. Dependency on a chemical substance to avoid problems is a complete loss of freedom. God is left out of the picture. This is not what God wants for us. For a Christian to use a chemical substance in order to avoid problems means he or she is giving up letting God control the problem. Peter says it well: "Cast all your anxiety on him because he cares for you" (1 Pet. 5:7). Paul points out in Philippians 4:6,7 that we are to be anxious (worried or fearful) about nothing, but in any and every circumstance take our problems to God in prayer. God will provide us with His peace. God wants to be the controlling force in our lives. We are God's temple and His possession (see 1 Cor. 6:19,20). Any and all use of His property is to be for His honor and glory.

Medical Purposes

Doctors prescribe drugs to help people with their illnesses. The Bible makes a few medical recommendations of its own when it comes to intoxicants. King Lemuel received excellent advice from his mother regarding the use of alcohol; she told him that a person in leadership should avoid drinking (see Prov. 31:4,5). Craving alcohol leads to poor judgment and corruption. The passage goes on to say that wine does have some medicinal use. A person who is perishing, or in great pain physically, needs something to relieve the hurt (see v. 6,7). Wine does have the ability to numb the emotional and physical pain of the suffering and even helps them forget their misery for a time (see v. 7). Doctors don't use wine for these purposes anymore, but they used to do so.

Paul may have talked with his own physician, Dr. Luke, about Timothy's stomach disorder and frequent ailments, for we find the apostle advising the younger man to use some wine for his stomach (see 1 Tim. 5:23). This medical use could have been in order to aid Timothy's digestion or to relieve some pain he experienced in his body. The Romans used gall, possibly an opium drug, to relieve the pain of those on the cross (see Matt. 27:34). The good Samaritan used wine with oil in order to treat the wounds of the stranger (see Luke 10:34).

RESPONSIBLE USE OF DRUGS

In looking at intoxicants we have found that we are to use them responsibly. A philosophy for responsible use might include the following points:

1. We should recognize what substances are drugs and be aware of what they can do to our bodies.

2. We should be able to separate ourselves from a drug. Dependency and addiction to any substance are sure signs of a lack of responsibility.
3. We should be conscious of any adverse effects of drugs upon our health or behavior.
4. We should always use our bodies and our minds to glorify and please God.

As you think about your own use of drugs, keep these points in mind so you can use drugs responsibly. Because the information in this study is not exhaustive, you may want to contact your local Health Care and Drug Education and Prevention agencies for added information.

Notes

1. Tom Morganthau, et al, "Kids and Cocaine," *Newsweek* (March 17, 1986), p. 58.
2. Ibid.
3. "The Myths and the Menace," *Listen* (October, 1986), p. 13.
4. "Marijuana," *A Scriptographic Fact Folder* (South Deerfield: Channing L. Bete Co., Inc., 1970).

Warning Signs _____

What are some warning signs to look for if you suspect someone close to you may be on drugs? Experts suggest the following signs:
1. Exhibiting non-social behavior.
2. Unexplained absence from the home.
3. Unacceptable behavior at work or in school.
4. Association with a new group of friends unfamiliar to you.

5. Indications of poor health, poor grooming or poor personal hygiene.
6. Jewelry or other valuables discovered missing.
7. Unusual supply of money or continual requests for money.
8. Possession of items associated with drug use.
9. A change in dress or jewelry to styles characteristic of the drug scene.

Although you may observe one or several of the above signs in someone you know, they are not always the result of drug abuse. Teenagers, especially, are experiencing physical, emotional and social changes that may result in erratic behavior or styles. But evidence of these warning signs should alert the observer to look for the possibility of drug involvement.

By Laura Wagner

2

Trauma in the Home:
Victims of Abuse

JUDY ALEXANDRE

It's nearly 5:30. The children slip quietly to their rooms and shut their doors. Mom watches the clock nervously as she tries to rid the house of any imperfection. She jumps at the sound of the car door. Daddy's home.

He's had a fair day at work, so things go smoothly until dinnertime. Then Jennifer can't choke down the lima beans, and Daddy's determined he'll not let her get away with that. "I told you to eat your dinner, you little whiner. Are you gonna eat it, or am I gonna have to smack you?" She cringes, and he curses and throws his spoon at her in disgust. Mom puts her hand out—a silent warning to Jennifer not to cry—but it is too late. The tears slide down her face, and Daddy grabs Jennifer up out of her chair to discipline her—a process that will leave welts on her body for hours, bruises on her body for days.

This is not a pretty scene. It is not a scene that comes to mind when one dreams of the traditional family. But it is not all that uncommon, either.

In 1984, physical, verbal and emotional abuse is reported to have happened to approximately 1,880,000 children *daily* in the United States.[1] Researchers estimate that one out of every three girls and one out of every seven boys will be sexually abused by the time they are eighteen.[2] ("Half of all sexual abuse of children occurs within the family.")[3] Another estimation: Somewhere between 2,000 and 5,000 children die every year from the hushed-up killer—physical abuse.[4] Unfortunately, abuse occurs in Christian homes as well as non-Christian homes.

Somewhere between 2,000 and 5,000 children die every year from the hushed-up killer—physical abuse.

The statistics are frightening. The implications, enormous. The day-to-day reality of trauma in the home seems to be a secret kept safe within the family walls. It's time we brought it out into the open.

WHAT EXACTLY *IS* CHILD ABUSE?

There are many definitions of child abuse, but one commonly cited is from the Child Abuse Prevention and Treatment Act of 1974 that describes child abuse as:

"Physical or mental injury, sexual abuse, negligent treatment or maltreatment of a child under the age of eighteen by a person who is responsible for the child's welfare under the circumstances which indicate the child's health or welfare is in danger or threatened thereby."[5]

To clarify this definition, let's categorize maltreatment into five types of behavior that are abusive.

Major Physical Injury

Any behavior that results in major physical injury is abusive. Major physical injury would include brain damage, broken bones, internal injuries, poisoning and burns.

Other Physical Injury

Behavior that causes minor cuts, bruises or welts is also labeled abusive. Non-abusive discipline leaves no marks on the body or the psyche.

Sexual Maltreatment

Most people realize that incest or intercourse with a child, or rape of a child, is morally *and* legally wrong. Other forms of sexual maltreatment would include inappropriate touching and suggestive remarks. An adult who appears unclothed in front of an opposite sex adolescent may subconsciously be trying to seduce the child. This is abusive behavior.

Emotional and Verbal Assault

Abuse is not limited to physical and sexual maltreatment. Assaulting a child either emotionally or verbally is also a form of child abuse. Constantly belittling a child (telling the child or otherwise communicating to the child that he or she is stupid or incompetent or worthless); habitually pushing a child away, rejecting him or her; confining a child in a restricted place, such as a closet; manipulating a child by threatening or attempting physical assault or using a child for economic gain are all forms of abuse.

Emotional Abandonment

The flip side of emotional assault is emotional abandonment. It is the parents' role to provide emotional support for their young, and when this is denied, an important facet of the children's growth is neglected. Withholding expressions of love or acceptance, being overly critical, or blaming the child for the parents' difficulties are all forms of emotional abandonment—child abuse.

WHY DOES IT HAPPEN?

Family Background
Often, abusive parents grew up in homes where their parents were emotionally uninvolved, physically absent, abusive, involved in substance abuse or caught up in the world of success. People who grow up in this kind of environment often end up believing they are unimportant and not loveable. When it comes time to give to their own children, their emotional reservoirs are empty, and they have nothing to give. Their own needs are so intense that they look to their children to satisfy them emotionally. This is known as role reversal. Understandably, when children are given the responsibility their parents ought to have, trauma results.

Overwhelming Responsibility
Sometimes parents are overwhelmed by the responsibility of being an adult or a parent. In these cases, they may place more responsibility on a child than is reasonable for the age of the child. This is another example of role reversal.

Consider Jean. At the tender age of nine, she was forced to clean the entire house to her mother's perfectionistic standards. She was punished for things that were not in her control, such as not preventing her younger brother from falling down and getting dirty before church. The expectations placed upon her were too high.

Donna is another who was given more responsibility than

should be expected. As a child she had to bear her alcoholic mother's outbursts, clean her up and put her to bed when her mother was falling-down drunk. The child put the adult to bed, instead of the other way around.

Employment Difficulties

John was overwhelmed with his responsibility as the director of a large manufacturing firm. In order to believe that he could be in control, he demanded perfection from his family. Anything that went wrong was blamed on his wife. The children were expected to be perfect. Mistakes were not allowed. As the family became less able to function adequately under this type of expectation, John become more forceful and eventually began to push and shove his wife and belittle all the family members.

Unemployment or being under-employed can generate feelings of inadequacy, low self-esteem, a feeling of being a poor provider and sometimes the need to blame others. Anger builds, self-worth diminishes and emotional and or physical abuse may result.

Substance Abuse

Parents who are children of alcoholics or other substance abusers grew up in emotionally dysfunctional homes. They did not learn as children what is correct behavior, what are appropriate expectations or what is normal and healthy family life. They may create another emotionally dysfunctional home. Children in any home that has substance abusers will undoubtedly experience some form of child abuse.

Immaturity

Parents who are immature feel the need for immediate gratification. They expect instant obedience and response to their wants or needs. Children, being children, need to be handled with patience. They are not old enough, mature enough and smart enough to be able to give the immediate response demanded of them. Pain results.

Rigid Households

Sometimes parents, perhaps for one of the reasons mentioned above, enforce a household system that is both rigid and inconsistent. This creates confusion and chaos. Sue lived in such a home.

Her home was characteristic of many abusive homes—one where the rules were unclear, yet inflexible. Enforcement was based on the mood of the parent instead of on the child's own behavior. If Sue disobeyed, sometimes her behavior was ignored. Other times it warranted cigarette burns on her body. Sue never knew what would happen for what reason.

In Ephesians 6:4, Paul says, "Fathers, do not exasperate your children; instead, bring them up in the training and instruction of the Lord."

Child abuse usually happens because parents have had bad parenting themselves, because they are unable to handle stress, or because they are abusing a chemical substance. There are few parents who deliberately set out to hurt a child and inflict suffering.

WHAT DOES THE BIBLE SAY ABOUT CHILD ABUSE?

In Ephesians 6:4, Paul says, "Fathers, do not exasperate your children; [RSV: "do not provoke your children to anger"] instead, bring them up in the training and instruction of the Lord." The key here is train them; don't abuse them.

The New Testament is packed with instructions to be loving,

gentle, self-controlled, peacemakers. The Old Testament gives a beautiful picture of a parent loving the child, teaching him to walk, healing him, feeding him, leading him with kindness and love (see Hos. 11:1-4). The Old Testament ends with God's statement that either the hearts of the fathers will turn to their children and vice versa, or the land will be cursed (see Mal. 4:5,6).

Jesus is very emphatic in his concern over the young. "Whoever welcomes one of these little children in my name welcomes me" (Mark 9:37). A verse that would cause anyone to think twice is Mark 9:42. Jesus says, "And if anyone causes one of these little ones who believe in me to sin, it would be better for him to be thrown into the sea with a large millstone tied around his neck." God did not give us children to be victims of our frustrations. He gave them to us to love.

HOW DOES AN ABUSED CHILD RECOVER?

Children of trauma have been damaged. Instead of growing under the parental care God would like them to have, they have been stunted in the way they feel about themselves and about others. Abused children often find it difficult to trust anyone. They have a hard time accepting the fact that they are worthy of being loved by God and other people. They may feel responsible for the abuse their parents inflicted on them and may face a period of denying that their homelife was bad. They feel alone, isolated. Children of trauma find it difficult to give and receive love, because they fear rejection, abandonment or abuse.

To recover from this low self-image and mistrust of others, there are several things they can do. Understandably, healthy relationships are difficult for them.

Talk About the Trauma

In recovery, the truth needs to be spoken. The purpose is not to blame the parent, but to validate perspective, facts, beliefs, confusion and feelings. Talking about the trauma allows for the recognition not only of feelings, but of losses experienced and needs not met. People who are raised in abusive or neglectful homes are often taught to suppress their feelings or that their feelings are wrong. Expressing these feelings and having another respond, "Yes, I would have felt that way too" or "I can understand why you were scared" helps the victim realize that his or her feelings are not unreasonable. This is what is meant by "validating perspective." Parents who have been abusive often refuse to accept responsibility for the losses their children suffer. These parents may speak euphemistically about their own behavior or fall into a familiar pattern of blaming the child. A verbal or physical beating is explained away with, "I warned you not to bother me when I first get home from work." An embarrassing scene caused by a parent's substance abuse becomes "having a few drinks and getting jolly." The victim needs support in finding the truth about situations and discovering the losses it cost him or her—losses such as the ability to trust or be intimate with others, the loss of a carefree childhood, of self-esteem, of love. Recognizing these losses can help the people who were abused understand why they react certain ways. Eventually it can help them learn to compensate for or grow past the damage done to them.

Get a Support Group
Recovery from trauma will be helped along by adopting a network of people who are accepting—a group that will allow for the testing of new behaviors and the expression of feelings that are new to the individual.

Replace Old Messages
Old messages about worthlessness, denial and being responsible for parental abuse (emotional, physical, sexual) will need to be replaced. To truly believe in these new thoughts and feelings,

the individual will need to hear and to repeat the newfound truth. Continual repetition of what is true will take time and encouragement from others.

Meditate on Scripture

It is essential for the abused person to meditate on Scripture that reinforces the truth that he or she is a child of God and dearly loved. Growing in Christ allows for hope, forgiveness and also for a process of continual healing.

Come to Terms with Parental Behavior

Help is often needed in sorting out how to honor parents who have been abusive—how to honor them and still maintain personal integrity. It is necessary for the child of trauma to separate the parents' destructive behavior from the feeling that the parents deliberately desired to hurt the child. It is very important for the person to acknowledge anything the parents did that was good, no matter how little that was. The victim needs to understand that the parents' behavior stemmed from their own inadequacy and weakness, often caused by illness or pain in their own childhood. In most cases, it was not deliberate.

Learn to Meet Needs

Learning how to get their needs met and how to meet the needs of others in mutually beneficial and healthy ways is another step in the process of recovery. This involves clear and straight communication, the acceptance of others, the recognition that one is not alone and that one has the ability to give. This is learning to become a whole person.

WHAT CAN THE CHURCH DO?

It is probably obvious that the child of trauma will need help to recover from the mental and emotional scars of abuse. Christians can aid in this process by doing the following:

1. Be supportive. This can take many forms. It can be praising a victim for seeking help or referring the victim to a competent counselor. Support can take the form of any loving gesture that communicates "I care" or "I'm pulling for you." Some congregations sponsor counseling centers or provide facilities for group meetings such as those of Adult Children of Alcoholics.

2. Be a good listener. Listen actively by responding, if only by nodding. Respond honestly. If you cannot say, "I know how you feel," say, "It's difficult for me to even comprehend how you must have felt." Do not imply the victim was somehow responsible by asking, "Why didn't you *do* something?"

3. Let the victims know their feelings are reasonable. When victims share feelings of shame, distrust, anger, pain or emotional numbness, a simple, "I can see why you feel that way" tells them they're OK. Social customs make many people feel that any unpleasantness must be excused or kept secret. This is very counterproductive for victims of abuse. Victims need to face reality and deal with the truth of what has happened to them. Facing the truth helps free them from a distorted past.

4. Provide a sense of what is normal. Normal behavior can be modeled or it can be verbally communicated. The church can sponsor seminars or film series that teach family skills that were not practiced in the homes of victims.

5. Let them know they are loved (by you, by God). Expressions of love may take the form of including the person who has been abused in a group outing, sending them a card, calling to see how they're doing or simply telling them sincerely, "God loves you and so do I." If victims are of the opposite sex, care must be taken in keeping these expressions of love appropriate and understood. Remem-

ber, victims may not have any experience with normal loving relationships and may be very emotionally needy. Frankly state that your love is given as a friend if you do not want it to be taken as a romantic gesture.

6. Let them know they are valuable. Value is not affected by background, by what they see as their shortcomings or by what they have or have not accomplished. It is intrinsic. It is a part of being created by God in His image.

Encouraging and helping children of trauma will eventually bring them to the point where they can forgive the pain that was inflicted on them. It will also eventually bring them to the point where they can accept their own uniqueness as created by God—accept the fact that they are valuable and loved.

Notes

1. National Center on Child Abuse, United States Department of Health and Human Services, 1985.
2. Eugene C. Roehlkepartain, ed., *The Youth Ministry Resource Book* (Loveland, Colorado: Thom Schultz Publications, 1988), p. 180.
3. Ibid.
4. *Youth Worker Update*, Feb. 1988, p. 4.
5. Public Law 93-247, 93 Congress, Senate 1191, 1974.

If You Are an Adult Child of Trauma _____

Recently (August 1988, BFC Counseling Center), a group of adults molested as children answered the question, What would you want people to know about recovery? The following are their responses:

1. Let others know they *are not alone.*
2. Tell yourself the truth.

3. Talk to people; tell family members, spouse.
4. Acknowledge the symptoms. Acknowledge how your childhood is affecting your life as an adult.
5. Deal with and face the pain.
6. Let go of guilt.
7. Know what is your responsibility and what belongs to someone else.
8. Learn what is realistic child development. Observe children. Accept that you were a child.
9. Don't marry to fill the void and escape pain.
10. Don't expect others to change or to accept responsibility for their actions. You change for your own health.
11. Develop new alliances within your family. Talk to siblings.
12. As you grow you can give comfort and offer peace.
13. Accept the fact that trauma happens in "the best appearing families."
14. There is a hope and a future. God is real, a source of strength and able to handle any hurt and anger.

Guidelines for Effective Discipline _____

There is more to discipline than the proverbial rod. Discipline should first be teaching the child what should or should not be done. The next element is praising the child for doing or trying to do what is expected. Finally, use correctional punishment for intentional (never unintentional) wrongdoing.

Following are some practical tips from a child development educator, Barbara Marsh.

- A child wants boundaries and will keep asking for boundaries. A child is more comfortable when he or she knows what's expected.

- Think before you talk. Don't make idle threats or statements you won't want to carry out. If you say you'll do something, do it. Be consistent.
- Be fair. Don't expect more of your child than he or she is capable or mature enough to do.
- Don't ever label a child as bad. What children do may be bad, but the children are not bad themselves.
- Each child needs to be disciplined according to his or her individual traits or idiosyncrasies.
- Praise the child's good behavior.
- When you are disciplining, you need to ask yourself, "What am I teaching the child by what I am doing?"
- Hitting teaches a child to hit, or that adults hit.
- Spanking should be reserved for extreme situations (such as a child running onto the street, etc.) and then only on the fatty part of the buttocks.
- Removing a disobedient child from a situation teaches the child he or she can't be around other people if he or she can't behave.
- Loss of the child's favorite privileges can be an effective form of punishment.
- For the very small child, use distraction away from the potential problem.
- If you feel yourself getting out of control, get away, take a break, call someone for help.
- Show love to your child.

By Judith L. Roth

3

Homosexuality

DON WILLIAMS

There was a time in our culture when nobody would talk about homosexuality (sexual attraction for persons of the same sex). Then the lid blew off this subject. Gay or homosexual people went into the streets preaching "Gay is good." They identified themselves with liberation movements such as black liberation and women's liberation. They demanded full civil rights. They demanded full acceptance by the Church. They claimed, "God has made us this way. Our being gay is not a deviation from God's good creation but a variation of that creation made by Him."

Christians need to deal with the issue of homosexuality for several reasons. First, about 5 percent of the adult males and 2 percent of the adult females in the United States identify themselves as homosexual. Thus, there are numbers of gay people in our schools, churches and communities. Whether we know it or not, we are relating to them.

Second, many gays are advocating a "gay life-style" and claiming that there is no moral, psychological or spiritual problem with being gay. Even the American Psychiatric Association no longer sees homosexuality as a problem of emotional illness.

Third, many younger people are struggling with homosexual feelings. "What does this mean?" they ask, "Am I gay?"

Fourth, some professing Christians who are also homosexual claim that the Bible is not opposed to homosexuality as such and that all that really matters to God are healthy, monogamous, committed sexual relationships, whether straight or gay. This final point leads us to the heart of this chapter—what does the Bible really say about homosexuality? How are we to understand this human condition from God's point of view?

WHERE DO WE BEGIN?

The first issue we must face when turning to God's Word is: Where should we begin to read? Those who advocate that Christians who are practicing homosexuals should be fully accepted in the Church *as they are* begin their reading with the story of Sodom and Gomorrah in Genesis 19:1-29. They point out that this story refers to God's judgment upon Sodom for homosexual rape. Next, they rightly say that all gay Christians are also opposed to homosexual rape, just as heterosexual Christians are. Then they turn to the laws against male homosexual acts in Leviticus 18:22 and 20:13. Here they claim that these laws refer to male cult prostitutes and are there because of the idolatry involved in the cultic act. Furthermore, they claim that these laws are equal to other laws in Leviticus such as those against making cloth out of two kinds of thread, like linen and wool (see Lev. 19:19). Thus if we enforce the laws against homosexual acts, why don't we enforce the laws against mixing nylon and rayon?

Turning to the New Testament, gay advocates point out that

Jesus said nothing about homosexuality. If He was silent (it is supposed), He must not have cared about the subject. It is Paul, of course, who talks a lot about homosexuality (see Rom. 1:26,27; 1 Cor. 6:9; 1 Tim. 1:9,10). Homosexual Christians who advocate their gay life-style claim that Paul only knew about "perverts" (heterosexual people who commit homosexual acts) rather than "inverts" (people who never knew a time when they were not attracted sexually to the same sex). Thus, they claim, Paul has nothing to say to most homosexual people who have not chosen their homosexual orientation, but who have always felt their same-sex attraction.

Is it proper, however, to read the Bible in such a prooftexting way? Should we just look up all the individual references to homosexuality and then try to draw our conclusion? If we don't do this, what should our approach be?

BEGIN WITH GENESIS

Simply speaking, the alternative is to start reading the Bible at the beginning, namely Genesis 1. The advantage of this is that the texts on homosexuality will then be placed in the context of the whole of the Word of God. Jesus Himself follows this method when He argues against divorce by going back to creation, what God intended when He made us male and female and ordained the permanent bond of marriage (see Matt. 19:3-9).

If we start then by reading Genesis 1—2 what do we discover about the creation of human beings and their sexual relationship as God ordained them? Read these chapters and then consider the following points:

1. God made us in His image as male and female (see Gen. 1:26,27). He shows that His character is fully reflected only in a heterosexual community. God is not fully seen in a male-male community or in a female-female community.

2. God blessed heterosexual sexual union and saw as the

outcome the procreation of the race (see v. 28). Thus, biologically our genital structure is made for heterosexual union.

3. When it was not good for man to be alone, God did not create a second man but a woman (see 2:18,22). Same-sex relationships cannot assuage our created loneliness.

4. God's purpose in creation was that Adam and Eve be united in the monogamous, permanent, heterosexual sexual union of "one flesh" (see v. 24). This is impossible in same-sex relationships.

When we continue reading in Genesis 3, we discover that the goodness of creation has been ruined by the Fall (see vv. 16-19). It was the seduction of Satan as the serpent (see vv. 1-5) and the entrance of sin (see v. 7) that perverted God's original intention for our sexuality. Thus, we must conclude that homosexuality is not a result of God's good creation (see Gen. 1—2) but a result of its disruption in the Fall (see Gen. 3).

Homosexuality is not a result of God's good creation but a result of its disruption in the Fall.

If this is true, then it is no surprise that in Sodom (see Gen. 19) homosexual rape is a sin. Moreover, it is a sin for two reasons. First, forced sexual relations with anyone is a violent violation of the person. Second, same-sex relations violate God's order in creation where He made us for heterosexual union.

Now we can also understand why the laws in Leviticus 18:22 and 20:13 prohibit male sexual acts with males. They do so not because of the sin of cult prostitution (it is hard to see how homosexual acts can be related to the fertility cults around Israel) but because of the sin of corrupting God's order for our sexuality being expressed in a heterosexual union. Moreover, these laws are enduring because they express God's order in creation and are reaffirmed in the New Testament. This is not true, however, of the laws about mixing threads.

Here someone might ask, "But what about the law that those who engage in homosexual acts should be put to death (see Lev. 20:13)? Certainly you don't believe that this law should be enforced." The answer is, "Yes, those who do this should be put to death, along with murderers, adulterers, liars and racists." All sin deserves death (see Ezek. 18:4; Rom. 6:23). The good news, however, is that Christ has been put to death in our place. He has died for homosexual persons and heterosexual persons; straights and gays.

LIGHT FROM THE NEW TESTAMENT

Well, then, if the Old Testament is clear that homosexual acts are sin, why is Jesus silent on the subject? There are two answers to this question. In the first place, Jesus didn't address homosexuality because it was not an issue among the Jews. They experienced little or no homosexuality. It was only in the Greco-Roman world that homosexuality was practiced. Therefore, it was Paul who had to deal with it, not Jesus.

In the second place whenever Jesus did speak about human sexuality, He always presupposed heterosexuality (compare Matt. 5:27,28). Thus, as we have mentioned, when Jesus voiced His opposition to divorce, He went back to Creation for the basis of His argument and ruled out divorce because "it was not this way from the beginning" (Matt. 19:8). If Jesus had had to address homosexuality, He certainly would have made a similar argument.

When we turn to Paul, then we find the most specific verses on homosexuality in the whole Bible. In Romans 1:26,27 Paul speaks of lesbians (female homosexuals) as well as male homosexuals. The objection of gay advocates—that Paul knew nothing of "inverts" (those who have always been attracted to the same sex) contains an element of truth. Paul viewed all homosexual acts as a perversion of human sexual relations. He did so, not because he was ignorant of modern psychological data, but because of Genesis 1—2. Because God created us for heterosexual relationships, all homosexual acts, be they by "perverts" or "inverts," are sinful. And they are a sign, as stated in Romans 1, of the wrath of God turning us over to our sin, the loss of human identity and the brokenness of human relationships in this world.

CONCLUSIONS

What then can we conclude from this study of homosexuality from the Bible?

1. Homosexuality is not a part of God's good creation but a result of the Fall and sin's entrance into the world. It therefore disrupts God's original order for the sexes.

2. Homosexual *desire* should be viewed as a sickness. Same-sex desire, although not consciously chosen by a gay person, is a corruption of the sexual desire that is created to be directed toward the opposite sex.

3. Homosexual desire (temptation) becomes sin when it is nurtured and acted upon (compare Jas. 1:13-15).

Homosexual persons come to Christ just as heterosexual persons do—by repenting of their sins and accepting Jesus as their Savior and Lord.

---

4. When homosexual desire is not acted upon, it is still a distortion of God's good creation and is guilt-provoking and damaging. Thus this continuing desire should be healed, and gays should be released from homosexual bondage. Judith MacNutt,

a psychotherapist, has had a 100 percent cure rate for homosexual persons through a combination of professional counseling and prayer-therapy for inner healing (the healing of past hurts and emotional damage).

5. Homosexual persons come to Christ just as heterosexual persons do—by repenting of their sins and accepting Jesus as their Savior and Lord. As new Christians, homosexual persons then need the healing of God in the community of the Church. The Church needs to keep its doors open to members of the gay community so that they might be recipients of God's grace. But we cannot welcome their homosexual orientation as in keeping with God's will for a Christian.

6. Those who have homosexual feelings need to know that this does not necessarily mean that they are "gay." In fact, God creates all of us "straight." Such feelings and fantasies may come and go on the route to sexual maturity. If anyone is troubled by these feelings, a professional Christian counselor can be of great help.

In the New Testament Paul speaks of sinners who will not inherit the Kingdom of God. These include homosexuals (see 1 Cor. 6:9-10). Paul then goes on to say, "That is what some of you were. But you were washed, you were sanctified, you were justified in the name of the Lord Jesus Christ and by the Spirit of our God" (1 Cor. 6:11). These former homosexuals and other former sinners now make up the Church. There is hope for the homosexual person in Christ. This is good news in our broken world!

4

AIDS: What We Should Know About It

The Christian singer pauses between songs. Blocking the stage lights from his eyes, he looks out on a thousand faces to explain that the next song speaks of God's judgment against sin. The audience is silent. He points out that every sin has its price. "Amen!" someone shouts from the crowd. "Sinful actions will be judged!" (More amens.) "And upon the wicked practices of homosexuals," he continues with vehemence, "God's judgment is AIDS!" Overwhelming applause. Ironically, some of the individuals clapping are carrying the AIDS virus and don't even know it. Yet.

Colleen, 19, is sitting in the front row. She got the virus three years ago by having sex with the young man she was dating. (He got it from sex with an old girlfriend who picked it up from a dirty needle the only time she ever tried speed.) Colleen has been having sex with her steady boyfriend, Roger, and now he is carrying the virus. Roger is sitting next to her in the crowd.

Phil and Vanessa are sitting a few rows behind them. They're married and carry the AIDS virus. Vanessa was a virgin when they got married. However, Phil had slept with a girl in high school whose old boyfriend was Haitian. (He had received it from a contaminated needle at a health clinic there.) Phil and Vanessa left their two-year-old son Michael with a baby-sitter tonight. Michael got the AIDS virus in his mother's womb.

Bob, 58 and a widower, is sitting with a group of friends from his church. He is now fully recovered from injuries sustained in a car accident that took the life of his wife. Only through major blood transfusions were the doctors able to keep him alive through the emergency surgery. Some of the blood he received was tainted by the AIDS virus.

Not one of these AIDS virus carriers is homosexual, nor has any one of them ever had a homosexual experience although some were guilty of sexual sin. But in the next four years or so, several of them will develop Acquired Immune Deficiency Syndrome—AIDS—and they'll have learned too late that the virus is no respecter of sexual orientation. Even those who don't develop the disease themselves will pass the virus on to others, who will pass it on to still others. The following results are sickening: Of those who receive the AIDS virus, between one-fourth and one-half will eventually develop the AIDS disease; death is almost certain. The United States Surgeon General, C. Everett Koop, reports; "By the end of 1991, an estimated 270,000 cases of AIDS will have occurred with 179,000 deaths [in the United States] within the decade since the disease was first recognized."[1]

AIDS is not a homosexual disease. The sexual habits of homosexual men make them more efficient transmitters of the virus, and so 65 percent of the known cases in the United States are homosexual men. But one-fourth of the cases are intravenous drug users, and one out of every ten victims got the virus through heterosexual sex, blood transfusion, an infected mother, or some undetermined method.[2]

Despite these facts, the Christian community has reacted to AIDS with energy unmatched. Some preachers, musicians and writers declare the disease as God's righteous judgment on homosexual sin. AIDS is the consequence for *them*—the gays, the bisexuals and the sexually perverse. *They* deserve it. *They* reap what *they* sow. Romans 1:26,27 is often used to justify this view of AIDS:

> Because of this, God gave them over to shameful lusts. Even their women exchanged natural relations for unnatural ones. In the same way the men also abandoned natural relations with women and were inflamed with lust for one another. Men committed indecent acts with other men, and received in themselves the due penalty for their perversion.

AIDS, many claim, is the "due penalty for their perversion." At first look, it seems that they are absolutely right. But a careful reading of Scripture shows otherwise.

Romans 1:26,27 mentions male and female homosexuals. Yet very few lesbians have AIDS. Does God practice sex discrimination by withholding women from judgment? And what about Colleen, Roger, Phil, Vanessa, Michael, Bob and the hundreds of other people who aren't homosexuals but have the "punishment"? Paul describes the penalty as a consequence that is unavoidable and is assessed because of immoral sexual conduct. How is it that some unrepentant homosexuals are not being punished while blood recipients and children born to AIDS carriers are dying from the disease? If God is passing out AIDS as the punishment for homosexuals, He is getting some of the names mixed up.

Homosexual behavior is not the latest fad in sexual trends—

it is as old as recorded history. Yet the first confirmed cases of AIDS did not occur in the United States until 1981. If this is the punishment Paul referred to 19 centuries ago, God has taken His time in dishing out the penalty.

Many other diseases and medical problems tend to attack a particular segment of society: Sickle cell anemia occurs predominantly among blacks; Tay-Sachs disease primarily affects Eastern European Jews; ten times as many men as women have color blindness. Are these groups being singled out for special punishment? Maybe acne is God's punishment to adolescents, diaper rash His penalty for the childish behavior of infants and constipation His judgment against old people who drive slowly.

In a way, all of these conditions are a part of God's judgment of a sinful world. Sin entered the world when Adam and Eve rebelled against God—the consequence was banishment from the garden, and the reality of pain, disease and death (see Gen. 3). And since we have done no better than those two when it comes down to obedience to God, we are partly to blame for the evil around us.

AIDS is not necessarily God's special, divine judgment on homosexuals. However, like all diseases that are primarily transmitted through sex, it can be the consequence of wrong choices.

AIDS is not necessarily God's special, divine judgment on homosexuals. However, like all diseases that are primarily transmitted through sex, it can be the consequence of wrong choices. But if AIDS isn't the judgment Paul mentions, what is? The Scriptures state that there is a specific penalty for homosexual behavior and that offenders receive the penalty "in themselves" (Rom. 1:27). Sin in all its forms changes us on the *inside*—it alters our self-image, destroys our self-control and drives a wedge between us and God. I believe the consequence of homosexual sin is the loss of sexual identity. The more homosexual experiences one has, the more severe the damage. Some individuals have so lost this identity that they believe they are men trapped in female bodies or women trapped in male bodies. And pathetically, a few disfigure these bodies, attempting to make their outsides match up with the distorted images they have on the inside. This loss of sexual identity, along with the rest of the changes that take place in one's "self" as a result of sin, are penalties far worse than any disease: AIDS kills the body, but sin and its consequences kill the soul.

AIDS is the leprosy of the modern age. Imagine being such a "leper." It's cold season, and you pick up a cold like you do every year. Only this time you don't shake it off in a few days; instead, it just keeps getting worse. Your doctor discovers a mild pneumonia; you're to stay in bed for a week and take antibiotics. Two weeks later you're not any worse—but not any better, either. You check into the hospital so that a trained medical staff can give you intravenous treatment and monitor your improvement. But for two more weeks all they can monitor is your decline. Your body doesn't seem to respond to the antibiotics, so a series of blood tests are taken. Then the doctor tells you why you haven't been getting any better.

There's a problem in your body's natural protection system that was supposed to fight off the pneumonia virus. Since the cold weakened your body, the virus was able to infect your lungs. But your immune system, fighting alongside the antibiotics, should have destroyed the enemy within the week. As it turned out, your antibodies never even showed up for the battle. The "command" cells (known as helper T cells) that were supposed to tell the antibodies where to go were destroyed by another virus that you've been carrying around for four years without knowing it. And since that virus (called HTLV-3) attacked the very cells that are in the business of killing viruses, your body is defenseless—a country without an army. In other words, you have AIDS.

Once you are diagnosed with the disease, your family and friends disappear; the fear of contamination taints every relationship. Those who do come into your room—doctors and nurses—speak through masks and touch with gloved hands. Like other terminally-ill patients, you sense that the hospital staff and volunteers don't want to grow too attached to you; it will be easier on them when you die if they lose a patient rather than a friend. When your roommate and other AIDS patients begin to die off, you realize that the only way out of this hospital ward is in a hearse. You are a modern-day leper, and nothing short of a miracle is going to keep you from dying as one.

Christ's treatment of the lepers is far different from the way we treat the similar outcasts of our day:

> A man with leprosy came to him and begged him on his knees, "If you are willing, you can make me clean." Filled with compassion, Jesus reached out his hand and touched the man. "I am willing," he said. "Be clean!" Immediately the leprosy left him and he was cured. Mark 1:40-42.

Christ looked beyond the decaying flesh to find a soul desperate for the touch of another human. This one act of compassion ought to make us ashamed of our selfishness toward the untouchable human beings in our own society. Because of our judgmental reaction to the AIDS crisis, Christians have given the victims a view of our Lord that is the antithesis of His true nature. We portray Him as an angry God who strikes down sinners with a deadly virus. But He reveals Himself in Scripture as a loving God who allowed His own son to be struck down to save those sinners. Rose Hernandez, a hospital nurse working with AIDS victims in the San Francisco Bay area, describes her first encounter with an AIDS patient:

Our head nurse said we would draw straws to see who would treat him because we were all making excuses for not wanting to become involved. I thought of the man's dignity and I volunteered to take care of him, remembering that the Lord was taking care of me. I was frightened. I wore double gloves, mask, gown, booties and hat. The patient was about 23 years old, of Haitian background. I remember the tears in his eyes as I held his hand in my gloved hand. He wanted to be accepted, to die with dignity. I asked myself, "How can I judge these people?"[3]

As Christians, we need to stop using our knowledge of the Bible to find proof of God's judgment on sin. Instead, let's use it to show people that Christ's love is greater than sin and disease. Ray Stedman, pastor and popular Bible teacher, puts it this way: "The world says to the victim of AIDS, 'You made your bed, now lie in it,' but Jesus' words to him are, 'Rise, take up your bed and walk.'"[4]

As Christians we can make a difference in the AIDS crisis by living out what Jesus would want us to do in the face of such a dark situation. Here are some ways adults can do that.

DEAL IN COMPASSION

In Matthew 25, Jesus tells a story of a group of people who, during their lives, fed the hungry, satisfied the thirsty, gave comfort to strangers, clothed the needy and visited the sick and imprisoned. He explains to His listeners that whenever they did these things for anyone, they were doing them for Him. There are few people sicker than an AIDS victim, and no one more worthy of our time other than the God who created him.

Feeling hopelessly rejected, many AIDS patients long to know that they are loved by someone. The knowledge of the desperate loneliness of AIDS patients leaves many Christians struggling with their obligation to love Jesus by loving the suffering out-casts of society (see Matt. 25:40).

When Pastor Lon Solomon of McLean Bible Church in North-ern Virginia received a call from a church member whose nephew—a Christian whom Pastor Solomon had baptized—was diagnosed with AIDS, he knew that he had come face-to-face with his ministry responsibility to the AIDS patient. Up until this time, Pastor Solomon did not think that the AIDS crisis would impact his suburban congregation in its affluent area. As a result of this call, his church began working with *Love and Action*, a new Washington, D.C. area ministry to AIDS victims. This ministry visits and counsels AIDS victims in hospitals and outpatient programs, provides "care partners" for AIDS patients and pairs them with area churches.

Seventy-eight of the eighty people that this ministry has been working with recently have received Christ as their Savior or have recommitted their lives to Him. Pastor Solomon is pres-ently discussing with his elders the possibilities of bringing AIDS victims into the church.[5]

American Red Cross president Richard Schubert stated, "Before long, *every* church of any consequence or size will have somebody in the congregation or on the periphery affected by AIDS, as will every work site and school."[6]

Many otherwise compassionate people are hesitant to get involved with AIDS patients for fear of contracting the disease themselves. The risk is much smaller than many realize. The AIDS virus is very fragile outside the human body, usually dying within seconds of being exposed to the air in a hostile environ-ment. Basic sanitary precautions should be taken: Avoid contact with body fluids and open wounds, and wash your hands after touching the patient. Always talk to the patient's doctor to find out if there are any extra precautions you should take. By find-ing out the facts, fear won't keep you from touching the life of someone who needs you.

STOP THE SUFFERING

You can keep others from getting AIDS by knowing the facts and telling others.

At the time of this writing there is still no cure for AIDS, and no vaccine to prevent others from becoming victims. Drugs being tested now have shown some promise in prolonging lives, but they work with only some strains of the disease, and they don't reverse the damage already done. Most of the people carrying the virus in their bodies don't know it since it takes up to five years for symptoms to appear. That means they will probably spread the disease to others. The World Health Organization projects that by 1991, 50 to 100 million persons may be infected worldwide.[7]

The World Health Organization projects that by 1991, 50 to 100 million persons may be infected worldwide.

It has been estimated that from 1 to 1.5 million Americans carry the AIDS virus. By the end of 1987, about 50,000 had been diagnosed as having AIDS and about 28,000 had died from the disease.[8] America is getting off easy when you look at the AIDS epidemic in central Africa. As many as 5 million are carrying the virus, and leading AIDS researchers estimate the death toll so far at several hundred thousand. And in Africa, the disease kills as many women as it does men. AIDS is an international tragedy. It has been called the plague of the 1980s.

Share the fact with family and friends that AIDS is spreading fast. Let them know that one doesn't have to be a homosexual or an intravenous drug user to get it. Tell them that when you have sex with someone, you are having sex with everyone that your partner has had sex with in the past decade. AIDS is going to be with us for a long time, but you can save lives by knowing the facts and telling others what you know.

PRACTICE FORGIVENESS

Because most of the AIDS victims in this country are homosexuals, most conversations on the subject eventually move on to discussions about homosexuality. For some reason Christians have taken this particular sin and drawn more attention to it than just about any other sin common to man—and it's not as if there aren't any other sins to choose from. In fact, the Bible says that we have all sinned (see Rom. 3:23). Then it gets worse. Romans 6:23 points out that our sin is worthy of the penalty of death.

The great news of the gospel and the message of the cross is that we all can be forgiven of our sins. This is true for *anyone*, regardless of the sin committed. God is ready to forgive your sins—are you willing to forgive those whose sins make headlines more than yours? In *Christianity Today* Ben Patterson writes: "What we need, what all gays need is not a theory that says, in effect, 'I told you so!'—but a call to compassionate action. God met the evil of the world not with a theological analysis, but with a cross. So should we."[9]

The AIDS crisis has put Christians at the crossroads; the world is waiting to see which road we take. Will we allow millions to die while we applaud it as God's justice for sinners? Or will we reach out in the name of Christ and love those He chose to die for? Watch your step.

QUESTIONS AND ANSWERS ABOUT AIDS[10,11]

What does AIDS stand for?	Acquired Immune Deficiency Syndrome
What is AIDS?	A fatal disease that attacks the immune sys-

	tem, leaving the victims's body defenseless to illnesses that it can normally fight off such as pneumonia and meningitis.
How do you get AIDS?	Mostly by having sex with an infected person or by sharing needles and syringes used to inject illegal drugs. The virus is present in the blood, semen and vaginal secretions. It can be transmitted from one homosexual partner to another, or from a man to a woman or a woman to a man during sexual intercourse or oral sex. The virus can enter the body through sores in the mouth and microscopic tears in the tissue of sex organs.
How else is AIDS transmitted?	Some victims were exposed to the AIDS virus through blood they have received in a transfusion. Since the start of careful blood screening tests, this rarely occurs now. About a third of the babies born to mothers with AIDS are infected.
Can you get AIDS from shaking hands, hugging, kissing, coughing, sneezing or eating food prepared by someone with AIDS? Can you get it through masturbation, toilet seats, door knobs or insect bites?	No known cases have been transmitted in any of these ways.

Can you get AIDS by having your ears pierced?	No one is known to have received it this way as yet, but it is conceivable. If you are having this done, insist on a sterile needle.
Can you get AIDS from someone who doesn't know he or she has it?	Yes. This is usually what happens. Because it sometimes takes five years (and possibly longer) after exposure for symptoms to appear, most carriers don't discover they have it until they have already passed it on.
Can you be infected with the AIDS virus and never get AIDS?	Yes. Between one-fourth and one-half of those infected with the virus will develop AIDS within four to ten years. Some say that the percentage is more like one-half to two-thirds.
How can I protect myself from getting AIDS?	Wait until marriage before having sex. When you have sex with someone, you are having sex with everyone he or she has had sex with for the past 10 years. And once married you and your spouse must practice faithfulness.
Where can I find out more about AIDS?	Your local Red Cross office carries information, as do local and state health departments.

Notes

1. C. Everett Koop, Surgeon General's Report on *Acquired Immune Deficiency Syndrome* (U.S. Department of Health and Human Services, October 22, 1986), p. 6.
2. Kathleen McAuliffe, "AIDS: At the Dawn of Fear," *U.S. News & World Report*, January 12, 1987, p. 66.
3. Ray Stedman, "A Christian Response to the AIDS Issue" [seminar held at Peninsula Bible Church, Palo Alto, California, December 8, 1985].

4. Ibid.
5. "Churches Urged to Lead the Way in AIDS Care," *Christianity Today* (July 17, 1988), p. 58.
6. Dean Merrill, Bob Chuvala, "AIDS: What Do We Do Now?" *Christian Herald* (January, 1988), p. 23.
7. "The Extent of AIDS and Indicators of Adolescent Risk," *Center for Disease Control Morbidity* and *Mortality Weekly Report* (January 29, 1988), p. 11.
8. Ibid, p. 10.
9. Ben Patterson, "The Judgment Mentality," *Christianity Today* (March 20, 1987), pp. 16,17.
10. McAuliffe, "AIDS," p. 66.
11. C. Everett Koop, "AIDS: The Surgeon General's Report on Acquired Immune Deficiency Syndrome," *Los Angeles Times*, December 7, 1986, pp. 1-8.

Ways the Local Church Can Begin to Address Aids _____

1. Plan several Sunday evening, midweek or Sunday School sessions with AIDS panels comprised of members of your congregation interested in researching and presenting information. Panels can be planned to present: medical facts, education issues, legislation, ministry ideas and methods and other areas of concern. Choose people from your church to participate who are in the health care, legal, education or insurance professions who can address the issues from their perspectives, as well as concerned citizens interested in the issues.
2. Offer to participate in community education committees set up to recommend AIDS curricula for the schools and to help set policy.
3. Set up a community meeting with other concerned churches to address questions related to AIDS and how it will affect both the community and its citizens.

4. Contact a ministry in your state to people with AIDS, or to the homosexual or drug abuser communities. Invite them to present the ministry challenges and needs to your congregation. This can be done as part of a missions conference to focus on home missions.

5. Plan special meetings with your church young people to help them understand AIDS, how it is transmitted and their risks for contracting the virus. There are a vast number of resource films and materials available for teens that can be used for this purpose.

6. Hold special meetings with your board of elders, Sunday School teachers, trustees, deacons and other church leaders to begin discussing the challenges AIDS puts before your congregation and begin putting a plan together for response.

Compiled by *Americans for a Sound AIDS Policy*. For more information contact P.O. Box 17433, Washington, D.C. 20041; (703) 471-7350.

5

Bigotry

JOHN M. PERKINS

I want to look at how I have been affected by bigots, as well as some effects I have observed with the hatred and behavior of biased persons. First, let me define the term bigot as I see it. A bigot is a person who has an unreasonable and blind hatred towards any other person who holds an opinion or is of a race or creed that differs from his or her own. A bigot believes that he or she knows what another person or race of people ought to have, to be or to do. A bigot will not only hate but will turn that hatred into a certain amount of pain that can only be released when it is directed personally against those people who are hated. It seems that the situation is relieved and the bigot is affirmed if there is a strong group, race or class that agrees with the bigot's opinion or at least will follow his or her action against the biased group. So a bigot, then, is one who is full of internal hatred and pain but thinks that the pain is released when it is directed toward others, and whose drive and motivation are directed toward the ease of the pain. Bigotry is the compounded form of prejudice.

BIGOTRY IN THE BIBLE

One of the clearest biblical examples of bigotry is found in Acts chapter 12 in the actions of King Herod. Here we see a sudden, violent eruption of hostility towards the Christians with seemingly no cause except that Peter was now accepting Gentiles into the Jewish-Christian church. This new command from God began to stir up a lot of trouble even among church members themselves (see Acts 11:1-3). But the bigoted non-Christian community was even more alarmed. Remember, the Jews hated the Gentiles. As long as the early Church was almost entirely Jewish, the Jewish authorities would let it exist in peace, for the most part, with only an occasional expression of hostility.

A bigot, is one who is full of internal hatred and pain but thinks that the pain is released when it is directed toward others, and whose drive and motivation are directed toward the ease of the pain.

But when it became obvious that the Church was accepting Gentiles into its ranks, this was too much for both the Jewish population as a whole and the Jewish authorities. So in Acts chapter 12, King Herod decided to make a show of his power by executing James the apostle (see v. 2). This was just a test case, a trial balloon. If the people objected, he would allow the whole matter to simmer down. But because the people were pleased (see v. 3), Herod went on to put Peter in jail, planning to execute him later.

Here we see that Herod's hatred for the Gentiles turned into pain that he wanted to release against the Gentiles. When the other Jewish people supported his efforts, he increased those efforts. The remainder of the chapter tells how God interfered with this plan by sending an angel to deliver Peter from that prison. And even today God is looking for His people to stand up and allow themselves to be used as instruments of His righteousness and justice.

God's heart has not changed; His Word is clear to state that "God does not show favoritism" (Rom. 2:11).

Now let me share some examples of bigotry that I have experienced in my own life. I want to look at some of the effects that these experiences have had in my development and even possibly share my response to some of these situations.

"WHO ARE YOU THE DADDY OF?"

The earliest memory of such an experience was when I was a little boy five or six years old in our little town of New Hebron, Mississippi. Now my mother had died when I was seven months old, and I was raised by my grandmother who lived in a little sharecropper's shack a mile or two outside of town. There were no black people who lived within the city limits of New Hebron, except the cooks who lived in the back of the white people's homes. All the other blacks had to live outside the town limits, so going into town was always something to look forward to as little boys. We would usually end up talking with some of the white boys and interacting with them.

On one of my first visits, I remember this one white boy coming up to my cousin Jimmy and me. He wanted to ask us a question. He asked me, "Who are you the daddy of?" And as a five- or six-year-old boy, I answered him by saying that I was the daddy of Jap Perkins, who was my father. Jap did not live with us, but I knew that he was my daddy. When I gave this answer I remember how the white boys just laughed and laughed at me. I had thought they were asking me whose son I was, and it took me a long time before I understood that joke and why they laughed so hard at me. I think at that early age, the white boys had been taught and told that we black boys were ignorant and inferior. And my not knowing that I did not have a son, reinforced that bias to them.

I can clearly remember this very incident, and I guess that began to formulate in my own life some opinions that caused me to hate inside. Realizing that someone was trying to make me feel inferior and being uncertain about anybody loving me anyway, affected my opinions about myself and my race. Even at that point I felt that society had made us believe that white folks were better than us because the material possessions they had around them were better. In our town of New Hebron, usually what people possessed was the basis for good and bad, and the bigoted southern white culture was dictating that philosophy without it being questioned.

Another incident from my childhood happened at the bus station in Columbia when I went to visit my father. Now this was a great event to travel 50 miles away from home. I was expecting and anticipating this trip for a long time, and I felt really special to get to go. This was my first time in a bus station, and I think my dad left me there briefly while he went outside to speak with some of his friends. But I remember in that bus station there were all of these black people in this dark back room, and I could look over through the window where I saw all of these white people in this nice place. But I remember that there was an old lady there, and I remember watching as she went out of our room to the other side to get a ticket or at least information from the ticket agent. The lady was nervous and afraid that she was not going to get the ticket that she needed, and she interfered with the agent while he was talking with another white person. This interruption caused the agent to turn around, and as we all watched, he cursed this old lady and threatened her like he was going to come over and beat her up and, in fact, said so. I was a little boy, and I looked around in that room expecting those men in that room to get up and to fight the agent for talking to this old black lady the way he talked to her. But as I looked around in the room, I saw those old men sitting quiet, some beginning to leave the room, and no one daring to confront him.

That made an impression on me, how that we as blacks were being so processed by bigots who had inward hatred. This man acted like he was mad and his search for his own affirmation caused him to release his pain toward other people. He wanted that room full of people to know who was boss, yet his hatred grew and could not be satisfied.

Even as a child I watched this behavior as I grew up in the South. I could always see the young white people wanting us to call them "Mister" when we would meet on the street. If we were ever stopped by a highway patrol or sheriff, they would shape their words in a way that you had to say, "Yes Sir," or "Mister." Most of the blacks learned how to live in that system. When we would see a white person coming, we would walk out the door and begin to say, "Yes Sir, Boss," or "Yes Sir, Mister," to affirm them. I would watch as many of those bigots then would turn around and really believe that they were loved by those black people who were simply trying to survive and get by in that system. We were supposed to make the white man happy; we were supposed to be "sambos," "jamup and honey" and "step and fetch it." Not only were we to make the white man happy, but we ourselves were supposed to be happy. And this constant struggle was what made the civil rights movement break out in the sixties.

It happened again when I was 12 years old. I remember seeing a white man from a nearby plantation busy hauling hay. The man was in a hurry to get that hay inside before it rained. He needed somebody to help him haul hay and I needed some money. So I took that opportunity to earn what I hoped would be $1.50 or $2. At least that was what they were paying for a day's work, and that's what I expected to get. I was thinking how great it would be to buy a new shirt or belt, or even a pocketknife to take home and show the other kids. So I went to work and worked hard all day.

In the evening I went to the white gentleman's house to receive my pay, and all I got was a dime and a buffalo nickel— just 15 cents. I had earned it, but at that point of anger and disappointment I didn't even know whether to take the money or not. Here was a white man handing it to me. I was in his house, I had worked for him, but I was afraid. Afraid that if I accepted the money I would hate myself because I knew my labor was worth more. Afraid too that if I didn't take the money, the man would say I was an "uppity nigger" or maybe a "smart nigger." And at that time in Mississippi, being black was bad enough, but a smart nigger was even worse.

So here I was all alone, my first time going out on my own in the workaday world; my first confrontation with a white employer; and my first face-to-face encounter with "the system." But, I couldn't do anything about it . . . so I took that 15 cents. However, I went away from there asking all kinds of questions. What had happened? How could that white man take advantage of me like that? My opinions and hatred were reinforced.

SATURDAY NIGHT IN TOWN

Then when I was 16 years old something happened that I will never forget. Daily life in Mississippi at that time was hard, but every Saturday evening all the farmhands would come up from the fields at noon, stop working for the day, clean up and head to town to visit, shop or just look around. Town was the real center of life. Town was also where the blacks and whites mixed and where the real hatred, bigotry and evil of the system came out. Of course the white man was boss and his system of law and order was simply to keep the blacks in line.

On this particular Saturday night, my older brother Clyde was taking his girlfriend Elma to the movies. Clyde was the hero to all of us younger kids. Clyde was like a second father; he had just gotten discharged from the army and we all looked up to him. But Clyde and Elma were standing in the alley, next to Carolyn's Theater, talking until the ticket booth would open. Nobody's real sure just what started it, but some folks think Clyde was kinda talking loud, maybe having an argument with Elma, when a deputy marshal standing on the sidewalk yelled at them. "You niggers quiet down." As Clyde turned to ask the marshal a question, the deputy clubbed him with his night stick. Clyde got mad and in self-defense, grabbed the marshal's club to keep the man from hitting him again. He struggled with the marshal and that did it! The law had all the excuse it needed. The marshal turned red in the face; you could see his eyes flash red. He was so mad that he shook. And before anyone knew what happened, he stepped back two steps, pulled out a gun and shot Clyde. Twice. In the stomach.

The whole way to the hospital in Jackson, Clyde's head lay on my lap in the back seat of Cousin Joe's car. Blood was oozing out, and I was quietly begging, "Brother, please don't die, please don't die." One and one-half hours later, we finally arrived in Jackson. After a long wait in the waiting room, one white person came out with the word that Clyde was dead!

Dead! My brother, my hero was dead, and anger filled my insides. All that fighting some place off in Europe didn't kill him; all that army talk about making the world a free place to live, and he had come home safe from the white man's war only to be shot down six months later by a white man in his own hometown. After the funeral it was all over. There was nothing more to be said about it. The bigoted whites would not question the authority or the town marshal, and many of the blacks lived in silent fear.

It's hard to describe. But when we spent our whole lifetime

with limited opportunities, spent our whole lifetime being told our place is at the bottom, we could not help but have a low image of ourselves. And after awhile our hope or anger or whatever it's called just sorta dries up, like a muscle that never gets used. What did it matter anyway? And within several months I got enough money together to go west. Maybe California could bring a better life. And it was in fact a good choice for me at that time.

To me the depth of what bigotry and racism had done to us as a black people in the South is reflected in terms of what we had to do to begin a movement that would begin to liberate ourselves at least from the legal segregation of the South. We first had to begin to affirm ourselves and our own dignity. We had to say to ourselves that, indeed, black is beautiful. Now normally it ought to be the behavior of society to affirm the other person's dignity and to give other people a sense of worth. We should be able to get personal affirmation from our friends, our teachers, our mother and family, etc., so that children will not have to grow up with the uncertainty of their worth or dignity as a person. But we had to begin by affirming ourselves of our dignity, because a whole society had been teaching the opposite.

Sociologists believe that the way such people will be healed is to direct their anger at the direct problem, and I believe that too. The difficulty comes in identifying the real problem. Most people will believe their problem to be other people, but in my life even as a boy I was able to see that the basic problem that we face in this racist society was an economic problem. The person that practices bigotry is believing the end result will be economic superiority. I truly believe that behind this bigotry is economics, and that in order to claim a piece of the American Dream these people must prove their power through the things that they end up possessing. Having money and wealth is the sure way to prestige, influence, praise and power. Through my observations of the system, I learned that lesson well. I found that my whole desire in life was to do that and to get that power. I was looking for my own affirmation, and I planned to get it through materialism.

MEETING JESUS

And then one morning at the age of 27, I was converted to Jesus Christ in this little mission in Pasadena. What really happened to me was that for the first time in my life, I recognized that I was loved by a holy God. I was overshadowed by God's love, and I was able to see for the first time my own sinfulness in the light of a God who loved me anyway. I found out that I could confess my sins and this good God would forgive me and accept me as His own. It was too good to be true; it was what I had been looking for all my life. So at my conversion, I gave my life to this God of love and decided to follow Him completely. I began seeking ways to organize my energy in such a way as to be able to follow God and His demands in Scripture, which is still my goal for today. That morning changed my life completely.

For the first time in my life, I recognized that I was loved by a holy God.

But the struggle didn't end there. After conversion I went back to Mississippi to live among those same bigoted people who had not yet found their personal affirmation, and it was tense. I guess for the first five or six years of our ministry in Mississippi, to a certain degree, I could avoid southern white people. As much as possible I kept myself somewhat aloof from them. But then if you were a black preacher in rural Mississippi, they sorta expected you not to interact with them, even though they called you "uppity." So it was easy for me to avoid the tense situations.

But as the sixties came along, I soon found myself having to be confronted, and I found that the pain was still there in my life.

I suspect that it was the night in the Brandon jail where God really began to push my own life past hatred. Twenty-three of us were almost beaten to death by the Mississippi Highway Patrol because of some civil rights activities in Mendenhall. That was the night that God gave me a real compassion for whites that I never before thought possible. When those men were beating us, brutalizing us, stomping on us that night, and on me in particular, I saw their pain releasing itself in cold hatred even beyond their own control of stopping it. I was trying to figure out the cause of that madness, and I was able to realize that their sin of bigotry had turned into a sickness or disease that poisoned their whole being. Hatred was eating at the hearts of these people like madness, and their faces were so twisted with hate that they looked like white-faced demons. For the first time I saw what hate had done to those people. These policemen were poor. They saw themselves as failures. The only way they knew how to find a sense of worth was by beating us. Their racism made them feel like "somebody."

When I saw that I just couldn't hate back. I could only pity them. I said to God that night, "God, if you will let me get out of this jail alive"—and I really didn't think I would; maybe I was trying to bargain with Him—"I really want to preach a gospel that will heal these people too." And by God's grace I did come out alive, but with a new call. My call to preach the gospel now extended to whites. I saw that they needed to be set free too. I began to understand that the same gospel that frees blacks also frees whites. You can't free one without the other, for our destiny is tied together.

Those lessons were not easy to learn. My beating and the frustration and bitterness that followed took their toll. Soon after, I had a heart attack and was hospitalized in Mound Bayou, which was an all-black town. After a partial recovery I found myself back in the same hospital with ulcers, so I had a lot to think about lying in that hospital bed. I though about blacks and whites and about how in a country that claimed to stand for "liberty and justice for all" a black man in Mississippi could get no justice. I thought about how in Mississippi, "Christians" were the most racist whites of all, how white preachers were in on most of the murders of civil rights leaders and how Sunday School teachers were leading members of the Klan. I thought of how the white "Christian" businessmen supported the whole economic system which exploited blacks. And there were times that I thought maybe there was only one way to go—to give up on whites and white Christians and just work for me and mine. It would be easier to just leave all that struggle behind us.

But when I was most tempted to give up, about to decide that the gospel couldn't reconcile—at least not in Mendenhall, Mississippi—two doctors administered healing to my spirit even as they cared for my body. A white lady doctor and a young black male doctor were themselves images of hope—living examples of reconciliation. And hope began to flicker again. Even when things looked darkest, when I most wanted to run, I couldn't get away from my new call: God had called me to take the gospel to whites, too. And I could really begin to see a healing process take place in my life. God was helping me to love people without desiring anything in return. God's love for me was now beginning to flow through me. How sweet God's forgiveness and healing were! I found them to be bigger and stronger than even hatred and bigotry!

A MAN OF THE MAU MAUS

I want to share one more example of an incident when I was able to see and review how bigotry affected people. It was in 1980 when my two sons Spencer and Derek and I went to Kenya, East Africa to spend a month. We spent most of our time living in the village of Kikuyu in the region from which the Mau Maus came.

I remember we were talking one day to one of the elders in the village who also had been an officer in Kenya's liberation movement. When we found this out, we wanted to know more about how this man became involved in the movement. So we visited him one evening. We spent all night there with a tape recorder and let him talk to us. He told us what made him a Mau Mau. A Mau Mau, or Kenyan freedom fighter, would do whatever was necessary to liberate the people. And this is what he told us.

This elder said that when he was a little boy they lived on a big plantation where his father was one of the house servants. All the kids in his family were also raised up to be house servants. He said there were hundreds of other Africans who lived on this giant plantation, but it was his father's job as a house servant to prepare the food and do the serving. One day as his father was bringing a platter of food and dishes to serve to the guests of their master, his father accidentally dropped the platter, and all the dishes fell. He said that the master took his father out into the back, took a whip and then whipped his father. He told us that he stood there and watched his father cry like a baby. There he was, a five- or six-year-old boy seeing his father become as a helpless man.

But this man grew up too and had to become a house servant because that is what he knew, and he was a servant for that same family. But by now the liberation movement in Kenya had begun, and he would hear about meetings that would be off in the forest some place. In order to join the Mau Maus they had to go to these meetings. So he went to one of those meetings, and there he heard the talk about liberation and about how they could be men. This leader told how they didn't have to be children anymore. The European society had made the African males as boys, children and second class citizens; now they needed to stand up and be men. The group was told what it would take to be men and to throw off that inferiority. The leader said that if they wanted to join the Mau Maus as part of his liberation movement, they had to go back and kill their masters' families, and then when they did that they could come back and join the Mau Maus.

The men then took a large cup, and they cut their wrists and allowed so much blood from their wrists to run into that cup, until the cup was full of blood from the people who were in the room. Then they stirred that blood, and they all drank it together. That was the oath that one had to take, and the idea was that they had all been joined together by blood; the only thing that would separate them now was death. If anyone went out and shared any information about the movement, he was as good as dead. This old gentleman said he left that evening and went out and killed his masters and their families. Then he went out and joined the secret society of the Mau Maus. He also said that this was the first time he ever shared this story with anyone.

NEEDED: GOD'S LOVE

And again, I saw firsthand the deadliness and the hatred of bigotry and what it can do to people. I believe that the only real cure for hatred and bigotry is that we as individuals respond in obedience to God's Word. We do have a responsibility, and we as individuals can respond by loving, caring and affirming the dignity of those we meet.

But also, we must create a community of people where that affirmation takes place. That is one of the greatest needs in northwest Pasadena where I live. We need to become a people who can soak up the hatred and anger of society, and let them end with us instead of reacting to them and passing them on to others. We need not respond to the hatred and violence with more hatred and violence, but rather penetrate that cover with love and compassion and concern. And of course that takes

God's love and power at work inside of us!

In closing, think about the needs and opportunities for a ministry of reconciliation in your own community. Determine what two groups of people in your community might have the greatest need for reconciliation. What part can you play?

6

Interracial Dating and Marriage: Is It Biblical?

JON TROTT

We were at the Great America Amusement Park with our kids, just having a good time. All of a sudden it seemed like everyone we passed was staring at us and whispering. All these suburban white families were gawking at my husband's black skin and at our kids and me like we were from another planet. I wanted to go home.

Western civilization has a dark, sometimes violent past when it comes to racism. In the United States blacks have been enslaved, Indians have been massacred, and Chinese workers have been picked out to be the victims of robbery and murder. During World War II Japanese Americans were put in detention camps.

Similar examples could be cited for many other "civilized" Western nations.

But many if not most people think that racism is a thing of the past. As one recent movie character put it, "Racism? This is the Cosby decade!"

Most racists won't stand out in a crowd. They can be very polite, kind people. Few would call a black person that word that is a profane twist on the word Negro. All would smile at a Hispanic baby. But where the "rubber meets the road" for the average person who considers himself or herself free from bigotry is in the area of interracial dating and marriage.

Racism is a heart condition, not a head condition. And only Jesus can change a heart.

Often, friendship is more rewarding and less risky than the dating game. Friendships are where communication across racial lines should and usually does begin. But what if things move from friendship to romantic interest?

A young black man at the office and I seemed to hit it off from the start. We would often go on breaks together and seemed to share the same interests. I was beginning to develop a real fondness for him. I don't know if another employee made a remark about us that he overheard, but he just never seems to be around at break time any more. I'm feeling some resentment and a little hurt.

What is racism? Webster's dictionary defines it as "a belief that race is the primary determinant of human traits and capacities and that racial differences produce an inherent superiority of a particular race." Whew. Not too appealing.

Think about someone you know who's addicted to alcohol or drugs. It's hard to understand the addicted person's actions when you're not addicted yourself, isn't it? But what about getting drunk once in a while? Or smoking a little pot? If the situation is right, even a Christian can yield to this sort of temptation.

The same thing can happen with racism. People like those in the Ku Klux Klan and other extremist groups are the junkies or peddlers of racism. But normal closet racists don't run around in sheets any more than the occasional drunk goes around exhibiting his or her weakness. The closet racist may even be unaware of the subtle control prejudice has over his or her thoughts and actions.

All the gentle reasoning or angry shouting in the world won't bring racists around. In short, racism is a heart condition, not a head condition. And only Jesus can change a heart.

RACISM AND SCRIPTURE TWISTING

How should a Christian view interracial dating and marriage? On any question of importance, the Scriptures themselves should be the focus of our search for an answer. What does God's Word have to say about marriage and romantic relationships in general? And even if Scripture gives interracial relationships the okay, what about the pressures society will put on them? Is it selfish or foolish to enter into such a relationship?

A few of the classic arguments against so-called miscegenation (a fancy, negative word to describe a marriage between two persons of different races) are Bible-based—supposedly. Keep in mind that the culture that invented many of these theories was one that had to come up with "moral" reasons to support slavery.

An important passage segregationists use from Scripture is the story of Noah cursing Ham's son, Canaan (see Gen. 9:20-27). Ham saw Noah lying drunk and naked in his tent. He went to his brothers and told them what he had seen. Instead of embarrassing their father further, the brothers put a garment over their shoulders and backed into Noah's tent, covering him without looking at him. For Ham's shameful behavior Noah directed this curse against Ham's son Canaan: "The lowest of slaves will he be to his brothers" (v. 25). The punch line? Ham's children, according to racist tradition, were black and thus cursed by God to be slaves and a suppressed people.

According to Scripture (see v. 25), it was only Canaan who received the curse, not Ham's other three sons—Cush, Mizraim and Put. Now the descendants of Canaan were the Canaanites, a Caucasian (white) people who settled in Canaan, the territory that later was to become Israel's Promised Land. While Put did settle in Africa, and his descendants were the Negroes (black race), nowhere in Scripture is it implied that black-skinned people are under a curse and that those who oppress them are fulfilling Scripture.

God did command the Israelites, as they began to possess and settle the land of Canaan, to destroy the Canaanites (see Deut. 7:1-3). But this command was never given regarding Negroes. Nor did God grant the permission to enslave blacks or mistreat them in any way.

Another racist twisting of Scripture centers on Cain. According to avid segregationists, God marked Cain by giving him black skin after Cain killed his brother Abel. This well-known argument is still used, despite the overwhelming rejection of it by Bible scholars. For although God did mark Cain in some way, the Bible doesn't even hint that this mark was black skin (see Gen. 4:15).

We can learn one valuable lesson from these examples of Scripture twisting: A reader can put things into a Bible verse or passage that aren't there in reality. In order not to fall prey to these twisted interpretations, each Christian should examine the Scriptures for himself.

MONGRELIZING THE RACES?

The real point being made by all of these segregationists' arguments is that there is a need to preserve "racial purity." They have found a way to reinterpret Genesis to support the idea that by mixing races we're contaminating God's creation. They say that God made everything to produce after his own kind ... kind means type and color or He would have kept them all alike to begin with.

How far can Scripture be twisted? The word "type" is actually meant to apply to species of animals and makes no sense if used to apply to human beings (see Gen. 1:24). All people are the same type, except for minute differences of skin, eye and hair color or differences of height and weight, personality traits and talents. If one couple, namely Adam and Eve, are the genetic parents of all people, how can anyone say people come in different types? Do skin pigments or facial characteristics matter to God? Furthermore, if God really wanted us to keep our skin colors pure, why not our hair and eye colors as well? Should blondes only marry blondes?

Another example of the "big twist": A common objection to intermingling of the races, or as some call it—"the mongrelization of the races," concerns God's Old Testament warning to Israel not to intermarry with the surrounding peoples. Many have claimed this refers to interracial marriages: "Miscegenation caused Israel to be judged by God." In this we see racial bias blinding people to the clear meaning of Scripture. Two separate issues, spiritual purity and racial purity, are confused here. God is concerned *only* with the intermarrying of believers with unbelievers. God's people marrying worshipers of false idols led to judgment, because when men of Israel married unbelievers, they usually began following the idolatrous practices of their wives (see Deut. 7:3,4).

The most bizarre theory offered by racists is the idea that

blacks are the offspring of demons. This groundless theory isn't worth further time. I mention it only as an extreme example of how far the Scriptures can be bent by those searching to justify their crooked beliefs.

"These people that say blacks don't have souls, that we can't go to heaven, well, that's something I won't even discuss," says John, a 36-year-old black married to a white woman. John, a believer for 12 years, anguished, "How far can these people go? Do they have the tiniest idea of how they make me feel?"

It is the racist who falls under God's judgment. He will be judged because of his idols: gods of skin color or other outward physical or cultural features. These idols are in direct opposition to the teaching of the Bible. "Man looks at the outward appearance," said God to Samuel, "but the Lord looks at the heart" (1 Sam. 16:7). All who accept Christ's Lordship are part of His chosen people. "There is neither Jew nor Greek, slave nor free, male nor female, for you are all one in Christ Jesus. If you belong to Christ, then you are Abraham's seed, and heirs according to the promise" (Gal. 3:28,29).

Those who oppose interracial marriage have based their arguments on an erroneous presupposition: Race matters to God. We can boldly state that it does not because of the evidence given us by Scripture. It is no accident that the Body of believers, the Church, is described as a human body, which cannot be divided (segregated) without harm to itself. No human being is less able to receive the Holy Spirit than any other: "For we were all baptized by one Spirit into one body—whether Jews or Greeks, slave or free—and we were all given the one Spirit to drink" (1 Cor. 12:13). That Spirit erases, or to put it more accurately, transcends the cultural/ethical/racial differences between people.

This applies to the final, and false, argument used by racists: Black, brown, white, yellow and red Christians can still be equal although separate. History shows us that where such a doctrine has existed, its practice has always led to the oppression of one or more races while lifting up another. Our most blatant modern-day example of this is South Africa's apartheid system.

"If you really keep the royal law found in Scripture, 'Love your neighbor as yourself,' you are doing right. But if you show favoritism, you sin and are convicted by the law as lawbreakers" (Jas. 2:8,9).

Being a respecter of persons is condemned powerfully by James: "If you really keep the royal law found in Scripture, 'Love your neighbor as yourself,' you are doing right. But if you show favoritism, you sin and are convicted by the law as lawbreakers" (Jas. 2:8,9). For a revealing study on Scripture's attitude toward discrimination in general, read the entire second chapter of James.

THE ONES YOU LOVE WON'T LIKE IT

There are no biblical objections to two believers of different races marrying. But that doesn't mean that interracial relationships are easy. In all my discussions with interracial couples, I found that the number one objectors to the couples' marriages were their own families.

Lyda, a soft-spoken white woman married to Ron, an equally soft-spoken black man, notes, "I think the main bigotry that we find is through our family. I have an aunt and uncle who have not spoken to me since my husband and I started dating. They even wrote a nasty letter when we announced our engagement. I think my family has been the main point of pressure we've experienced."

"Though it was no problem for us, it was for our parents," said Barb, a black woman married to Eric, a white man. "It was a question of how our children would be raised, what their racial identities would be and what kinds of persecution and pressure they would face." Barb paused to comfort her crying newborn daughter. "What we found out is this: Interracial couples make beautiful children.

"Our marriage has been used by God to help both of our families," Barb continued. "Eric's family never knew any blacks before me. My family has gotten an education too. My mom always disliked whites, but now Eric is around. He's not just 'a white man.' He's my husband, Eric. And that really has worked on my mother's attitudes. She wouldn't speak to me when we first got engaged. But then Eric's mom, who's a Christian and was also struggling over our engagement, got together with my mom. And that really got my mother thinking!"

Obviously, there are some points an interracial couple considering marriage should ponder carefully. Is the couple ready for the stares of passersby, some friendly, some not? Are they ready for that certain cool aloofness that surburban-bred Northern whites can turn on when disapproving? And are they ready for incidents like the one that occurred to one of my best friends, a white minister, and his wife, who happens to be black?

COULD YOU TAKE THE ABUSE?

Jason and Joanne (not their real names) were invited to a Christian friend's wedding in a Chicago suburb. But at the reception things turned anything but joyful for this couple. First, when Joanne, a black woman, approached the bride's mother, she was pointedly ignored. "I couldn't believe how rude she was."

Many empty chairs lined the various tables, but when Joanne's white husband, Jason, tried to seat his wife and himself, someone would inform them that the seats were taken. This happened once too often for Joanne. "Jason wasn't picking up on the stares we were getting. But I think as a black person, I'm more experienced in sensing bigotry."

Jason, to test Joanne's assertion, went to a table alone and asked if two places were empty; the reply was yes. When he brought Joanne to the table, however, a stunned silence enveloped the table. Then, quickly, the entire table of whites got up and left.

"There we sat, alone at this table . . . I just wanted to get up and leave," said Joanne.

The two sat alone until a group of hard-drinking people in the corner of the room asked them over. "We saw how those Christians are treating you," said one. "Come and sit with us black sheep over in the corner."

"Usually I'm not upset when people act like that," says Joanne, "because they're unsaved, so what can you expect? But when Christians act that way . . . well, I have a hard time thinking of them as Christians. I guess it's like any other area a person doesn't turn over to the Lord; you can be that way and still be a Christian, but before the Lord it's unacceptable behavior."

It isn't just white people who practice prejudice. Another interracial couple suffered at the hands of the wife's brothers, who felt that her "black purity" was being contaminated by her white husband. Before the marriage one brother even threatened to kill his sister and warned: "Your kids will have white blood. Don't you have any pride in your race?" She reflected, "There's a difference between black pride and black bigotry."

And in the splitting of the cultural hairs department, a Puerto Rican friend related to me his first experience with his wife's mother, a Guatemalan. "I wanted my daughter to marry someone from her own country, certainly not a Puerto Rican," she said to him bluntly. Though he could laugh about it in retrospect, he admitted, "I was really hurt by that. Funny, though, there are whites who look at both my wife and me as 'those latinos.'"

Henry, a Chinese Christian married to a white, believes his own race's problems here are more subtle. "For Chinese born in this country (the United States), the worst problem is our rejection of our own racial and cultural backgrounds. My generation wanted to be American, and that meant tossing out our own heritage. I refused, for instance, to date Oriental women, because that was identifying with Chinese culture. I was accepted by my white friends, but Orientals concerned with holding on to aspects of our culture were angry with me. Fortunately, because Christianity freed me from having to 'conform' to Western culture, I have learned to treasure my parents' heritage as well as this country's. When I felt the Lord leading me to marry Julie, a white woman, I didn't have to be introspective about betraying my heritage because I'd accepted the fact that my culture was a God-created part of me."

WHERE DOES JESUS CHRIST FIT IN?

The interracial couples I spoke to all said that their faith in Jesus Christ is absolutely the only basis for their marriage. "If I'd been a non-Christian, I'd have left John for sure," said Mary. "I was afraid of being an outcast and of people thinking I wasn't okay. I was afraid of him being black, because there was a lot in me that didn't want that stigma put on me. But once I became a Christian, I understood life from a whole different perspective; I understood what life was really about. I wasn't afraid anymore. I didn't have to worry about what other people thought, because it really didn't matter. What I was concerned about now was following Jesus."

All the couples I interviewed, especially black/white couples, emphasized the limitations of where they could live. "You want to find a place that's a mixture," says Erle, a black man of 39 years. "You don't want to live in an all-black area or an all-white area. Around colleges is good. When we lived in Chicago, Rogers Park was a place like that."

The couples I spoke with also said that the Church is their most important marriage support. Barb and Eric live in a full-time Christian community called Jesus People U.S.A. "Living in a full-time Christian fellowship," says Eric, "the racial issue becomes less important than it would if we were attending an average church, and far less important than if we weren't Christians. The whole issue of dating and marriage across racial lines is volatile—HOT!—when you do it in our still segregated society. In our community, race is a non-issue."

John and Mary were members of an otherwise all-black Christian community, and for Mary, the nonjudgmental acceptance she found from her brothers and sisters in the Lord was foundational: "Black people are more ready to accept an interracial marriage than white people. Even now, I have black women come up to me and tell me how beautiful my children are. I have never had a white woman—other than a friend—do that. I'm not trying to say blacks are better than whites, but because they've felt the pain of being oppressed and rejected themselves, I think they often are more aware of other people's needs for support.

"By living with black people—my husband and the other Christians of the community we were in, I learned things that most whites don't know. People are the same—good and bad included!"

What sort of lessons can interracial couples teach us? John says, "I feel like I have a mission to open people's minds, to say, 'Hey listen, we're just two people. Nothing more, nothing less. We're capable of feeling love and hurt and all the other things. In the fallen world we live in, a couple like us is going to be hurt and judged, but God brought us together; He'll preserve and strengthen our marriage despite the world's opinion.'"

PUTTING FIRST THINGS FIRST

How can a couple from different racial backgrounds know they are called to serve God together? Scripture commands believers not to be unequally yoked with unbelievers, and to ignore this command is to create a relationship or marriage that is full of pain and conflict. The bottom line, then, is to make sure both partners have the same desire to serve God. Pray together, get counsel from trusted older Christians. The foundational goals and aspirations of the Christian husband and wife—to serve God and to walk in His will—should be the same no matter what racial or cultural backgrounds are involved.

An interracial couple will experience a full spectrum of joys and frustrations. And, like any other couple, in times of stress they may go for the low blow, saying hurtful things. In these cases bigotry may raise its ugly head. Every husband, angry at his wife, has had at least the fleeting thought, "Maybe this was a mistake. Was I really listening to God when I married this person?" Thoughts like that come, and when resisted, go. But for two people already aware that society views their marriage as shaky, these thoughts can have added strength. It's surprising how racist such thinking can get: "She's so loud. So's her mother. All black women are loud." Or, "He's so cold and uncaring. Just like Mabel warned me; these white guys have no feelings." This isn't Christian thinking, but Christians sometimes think it.

On the deepest level, marriage is a miracle. As Scripture says, two become one. Without losing their individual identities, a man and a woman enter into a spiritual union that requires great sacrifice on both of their parts, but that also offers untold joy. No wonder God compares marriage to Christ's relationship with the Church: "The two will become one flesh. This is a profound mystery—but I am talking about Christ and the church" (Eph. 5:31,32).

The color of one's mate's skin and the cultural background the couple may or may not share have very little to do with a successful Christian union. Honest communication, plus the firm, single-minded resolve to a lifelong commitment are what a God-centered marriage is made of. All that is necessary—and it is absolutely necessary—is that both husband and wife are willing to obey God and grow in faith together, no matter what comes.

"What God has joined together, let man not separate" (Mark 10:9).

Friendship Only? _____

Sherrie, an attractive white school teacher, began dating Ken, a good-looking black man whom she, along with others, led to Christ.

From the start Sherrie was careful to tell Ken that she wanted the relationship to remain on a friendship basis; she had no intention of becoming romantically involved. Her caution was due to her observations of a friend's interracial marriage that presented continual problems and stress.

The family of Sherrie's friend opposed the marriage from the start and refused to let something good come from the union. Family members felt hurt and disappointed. They displayed their underlying anger by continually passing on information to their daughter and her friends about the problems of interracial marriages that they had received through conversations with others. Sherrie knew that she did not want to set herself up to become involved in a similar situation, although she felt that an interracial marriage was not prohibited in Scripture.

Even though Sherrie was up-front with Ken regarding her feelings, and he agreed to a friendship-only relationship, Ken, nonetheless, fell in love with Sherrie and began talking about the possibility of marriage. Acknowledging the change in Ken,

Sherrie broke off the relationship; of course Ken was hurt.

In retrospect Sherrie realizes that because of her decision not to become involved in an interracial marriage, she should not date a person of another race. This stance will prevent a situation being created where a fellow-believer can be hurt.

While Sherrie feels she is able to control her own emotions, she has learned from her experience with Ken that she is not able to control the emotions of a second person involved in such a relationship.

While the above case study is true, the names have been changed.

By Margaret Rosenberger

7

The New Age

TRACY L. SCOTT

"I don't believe in the God of Christianity. How can God be so remote, demanding and harsh? I believe in a loving Being who is part of me and everything else on this planet—a Spiritual Force which connects all of us together. We only need to realize our spirituality, and then we can be godlike and change this crazy world."

So my friend Miriam proudly told me of her faith in the New Age movement while we had lunch one day. And she made no secret of her dissatisfaction with Christian beliefs and the Christian church.

A few weeks after my conversation with Miriam, I went to visit Helen, a close Christian friend of mine. I told Helen about my friend, Miriam, and her New Age beliefs. She listened attentively and then replied: "You know, I'm not sure that Miriam is all wrong. I've been reading Shirley MacLaine's book, and I really like a lot of what she says. I don't believe the stuff about UFOs, but I do think she's really in touch with God in her own heart. She's much more spiritual than many Christians I know. She really experiences God, and she is so connected to other people and the earth."

I couldn't believe what Helen was saying. The New Age was enticing her, too. What exactly is the New Age movement? And what does the Bible have to say about this seemingly new phenomenon?

"New Age Movement" refers to a variety of organizations, people, beliefs and practices—not to a unified and highly structured institution.

I would guess that most Christians in North America today have encountered New Age influences, as I have, in various ways and among various friends. But there is so much talk about the New Age that it is difficult to sort out what it is and how Christians should respond to it. What I want to provide here is a general overview of some fundamental elements of the New Age movement, a Christian evaluation of them and suggestions on how to respond to this challenge.

WHAT IS THE NEW AGE MOVEMENT?

The term "New Age Movement" refers to a variety of organizations, people, beliefs and practices—not to a unified and highly structured institution. The New Age has no central organization tying all its diverse elements together. Neither does the New Age have any official leadership. Rather, the New Age encompasses many different groups and individuals who, while their emphases might differ, all share a common desire. They all want to see the world move into a *new age* of self-actualization and peace. And they believe that they can help bring about this new age through certain spiritual and social changes.[1] These changes usually include a rejection of both monotheism (Judaism, Christianity and Islam) and modern atheism.

Rather than believing that there is one Supreme Being or that there is no God, New Age adherents depersonalize God. To them all is god—reality is one ultimate substance. This and a blend of other religious beliefs have been borrowed and adapted from eastern religions.

This link to Eastern religions shows that the basic ideas of New Age movement are certainly not new. What is fairly new is the combining of these ideas without regard to their ideological foundations. This combining has its roots in a variety of religious movements of the nineteenth-century that rejected the Judeo-Christian view of the world. Transcendentalism, Theosophy, Christian Science, New Thought and Self-Realization Fellowship all promoted some form of eastern mysticism and occultism. This mysticism used ecstatic, emotional experiences to assert the "divinity" of humans and their "oneness" with God. The occultism referred to an attempt to uncover truths that are hidden from ordinary perception.

The eastern and occult ideas of these nineteenth-century movements were picked up by the countercultural movement of the 1960s and '70s. The counterculture was dissatisfied with the seemingly mechanistic and alienating culture of the West. They believed that the only hope for the future was to throw off established Judeo-Christian beliefs and realize the true unity and harmony of all reality. And the best way to usher in this new age of harmony was through eastern mysticism and occultism.[2]

Although most of the '60s hippies are gone, their influence is not. The New Age movement has taken over many of the myths and beliefs of the countercultural movement and brought them into the mainstream of American life. No longer are these views seen as musings of a radical minority. Rather they are increasingly accepted by many people in our culture. In order to stop the infiltration of New Age beliefs into our culture, we must learn to identify them and try to understand why they've gained acceptance.

WHAT DOES THE NEW AGE BELIEVE?

The specific beliefs of the New Age movement are undergirded by a basic world view that forms the foundation for other beliefs and practices. A world view is a group of assumptions, either conscious or subconscious, regarding what is real and true.[3] We all have a certain way of looking at life. This way of looking at life represents our world view.

Walsh and Middleton in their book, *The Transforming Vision,* offer a helpful framework for defining and describing specific world views. They say that a world view will answer four basic questions:

1. Where am I? (Or what is the nature of reality?)
2. Who am I? (Or what is the nature of human beings?)
3. What is wrong? (What keeps me from fulfillment?)
4. What is the remedy? (How do I find fulfillment?)[4]

Using this framework as a guide, we can learn about the New Age world view by looking at how the New Age movement would answer these four questions. And we can critique this world view by contrasting it with a Christian world view.[5]

Where Am I?

For the New Age believer, life takes place in a world of "oneness." Reality is best described as "all is one." Ultimate reality—or God—is impersonal spirit, pure consciousness or energy. This consciousness or energy permeates everything in creation. Thus all things are really of the same essence—all is one. The distinctions that we observe—such as between light and darkness, or between an animal and a person, or between God and myself—are not absolute. These things only *appear* to be different. The differences are not *real*.

Since God is the oneness (or unity) of all creation, then it follows that all things are God. All is one; one is God; all are God. Everything in the universe partakes of the divine essence.

The oneness of reality, so fundamental to New Age beliefs, is greatly opposed to a Christian view of reality. Christians find themselves in a world very different from the world as seen by the New Age movement. For Christians, reality is not single but diverse. Reality contains many different essences. The first and primary distinction in reality is between the Creator and the creation, as we see in the very first chapters of the Bible.

Genesis 1 tells us of a self-existent Creator—God—who created a world distinct from Himself. Although God is continually working in His creation, God is not contained in the created world: "God is in heaven and you are on earth" (Eccles. 5:2).

The oneness of reality, so fundamental to New Age beliefs, is greatly opposed to a Christian view of reality.

Genesis 1 also shows us that God created rich distinctions in His creation. God separated light from darkness (v. 4) and water from the dry land (v. 9). He created different kinds of plants and animals (vv. 11,12,20,25). And God saw all these distinctions as good (vv. 10,12,18,21,25). Thus reality is full of distinct objects and creatures and is fundamentally split along the lines of the Creator and the created.

Although reality is diverse, it is not fragmented. God provides a unity to the created order: "All things were created by him

[Christ] and for him" (Col. 1:16). All the diverse elements of creation "hold together" in Christ (Col. 1:17).

Who Am I?

Who am I? The New Age believer would answer resoundingly, "I am God." Since all of reality is God—God is all—then all human beings must be gods. As Shirley MacLaine advocates in her book, *Out on a Limb,* that to be fully human we must first realize that we are gods; divinity dwells within all of us.[6]

Thus, our task as humans is to perfect ourselves and achieve god-like levels of consciousness. Human potential is unlimited. Human nature is seen as intrinsically good. We fulfill ourselves and help the world by realizing this.

Who am I? The Christian would answer, "I most certainly am *not* God." To believe in human divinity is to believe the lie of the serpent: "You will be like god" (Gen. 3:5). Christians would identify this old lie as being the source of the delusion that leads the New Age movement to believe that humans are gods.

Acknowledging the Creator as the only true God, Christians realize their creaturely limitations. Human beings are created in the image of God (Gen. 1:26,27). We reflect that image as personal, thinking, feeling beings. But we are not part of God's divine essence. We are not self-existent, wholly good or all powerful.

Our task as human beings is not to self-actualize, but to worship God and to "have dominion over the . . . earth" (Gen. 1:28, *KJV*) in concert with other humans and in covenant with God.

What's Wrong? *and* What's the Remedy?

To followers of the New Age movement, the problem with humanity and the world is not sin but ignorance. They believe that we are afflicted with a fragmentary understanding of reality. To them, the scientific mind-set of Western culture and the Christian notion of sin have focused too much on human limitations. We are blind to the essential oneness of all things and to our own divine potential.

To remedy this wrong the New Age prescribes a new awareness of the One through new experiences. We can be transformed by these experiences and by connecting with everything else in the world that realizes the One.

The experience of oneness is brought about through various techniques that are applied to body (such as yoga), mind (visualization of images) and spirit (folk magic). The aim of these techniques is to alter consciousness so that it experiences the unity of reality. Only then can humans begin to realize their godhood and attain spiritual power.

New Age adherents also believe that personal transformation will lead to global transformation. By becoming more divine, humans will have the power to transform the world into the peaceful, unified reality that it is meant to be.

For Christians, sin, not ignorance, is the problem facing human beings. Adam and Eve were created as free beings able to choose either to love and worship their Creator or to rebel against Him (see Gen. 2:16,17). But the serpent came along tempting the humans: "You will be like God," he said (Gen. 3:5). The man and the woman turned their trust away from God in their desire to be gods themselves. God, as Creator, has legitimate authority over His creation. But the humans denied God's rule because they wanted to rule themselves. They chose to disobey God and usurp His divine authority.

This human tendency to sin has continued. The apostle Paul, writing of humanity's wickedness stated, "For they exchanged the truth of God for a lie, and worshiped and served the creature rather than the Creator" (Rom. 1:25, *NASB*). In his great letter to the Romans, Paul pointed out that sin, fundamentally, is this idolatry.

Likewise the whole human race cannot avoid the temptation to trust in themselves rather than in God. "For all have sinned and fall short of the glory of God" (Rom. 3:23). We would all like to think that we are perfect and godlike. We would like to believe the lie of the serpent, the lie the New Age has taken over—that of believing that the only thing wrong with us is ignorance of our own divinity. But the truth is that we did not create ourselves and cannot perfect ourselves. We are answerable to our Creator.

As the Fall in Genesis 3 resulted in consequences of hardship and death (Gen. 3:14-24), so our continued sin yields evil consequences and death. Willingness to trust and worship creaturely things will separate us from God. This separation is a form of spiritual, and eventually eternal, death (see Isa. 59:1,2; Rom. 6:23).

So what do Christians believe is the remedy for sin that perverts not only human beings' characters but also their task of having dominion over the earth? Repentance and faith in Jesus Christ, true God and true man, Savior of the world. "God made him [Christ] who had no sin to be sin for us, so that in him we might become the righteousness of God" (2 Cor. 5:21). When we recognize our own sinfulness, turn away from it and redirect our trust to God in Christ, then we will be saved from the results of sin—death (Acts 16:30,31; see John 3:16; 1 Cor. 15:22).

Finally, Christian transformation is part of the remedy for the basic ills of the world. Jesus Christ brings transformation to both humans and the world. Even now Christ is working in believers' lives to transform and redeem them. "Therefore, if anyone is in Christ, he is a new creation" (2 Cor. 5:17). All death and destruction and evil will be overcome by Christ when He returns. The world will be transformed; not destroyed but reshaped (see Isa. 60; Rev. 21:1-8,22-27; 22:1-5). Those people who have believed in Him will be resurrected and transformed. "In a flash, in the twinkling of an eye, at the last trumpet . . . . the dead will be raised imperishable, and we will be changed" (1 Cor. 15:52).

Thus, Christianity offers a hope and a vision for the future while it gives us the strength to persevere in the present.

WHAT CAN WE CONCLUDE
ABOUT THE NEW AGE MOVEMENT?

There are so many different aspects, beliefs and practices of the New Age movement that it is difficult to offer a comprehensive list of Christian objections. Yet we have seen that a general world view underlies the specifics of the New Age. And we have also seen that this world view is radically opposed to a biblically based Christian world view.

World View is the key to evaluating almost any aspect of the New Age we encounter. We must ask what is behind a specific belief. What does the belief say or imply about Who I am, Where I am, What's wrong or What's the remedy?

For example, reincarnation says that people have many different lives. What does this say about the nature of human beings? Reincarnation denies the finality of death. Death is not seen as an evil consequence of sin, but rather a gateway to a new life. Thus, with no ultimate consequence for sin, the inevitable sinfulness of human nature can be denied. Given enough lifetimes, humans can perfect and thus save themselves. This is the first step toward worshiping ourselves rather than God.

This example leads us to an important general evaluation of the New Age movement. Although the movement is diverse and complex, almost all of its elements are based on the world view assumption that humans can control their own lives, or that humans have some sort of divine potential. Most often our negative criticisms of the New Age will focus on this basic violation of the Creator/creation distinction.

As Christians, we fundamentally recognize God's divine sovereignty as Creator and our dependence on Him as part of His creation. Human beings are not God, nor will we ever be. This truth is at the heart of the differences between Christianity and the New Age movement.

Besides the world view evaluations, I can offer a few more

general comments about the New Age. On the negative side we must beware of anything that promises spiritual power apart from Jesus Christ. The miracles and magic of the New Age can come from no other source than Satan. If there are supernatural occurrences going on, they are not the workings of our Creator but are detestable to Him (see Lev. 19:26,31; Deut. 18:10-12).

On the positive side we must realize that the New Age is not a unified conspiracy but a mix of groups and individuals who are seeking answers to important questions. Many of these people are disillusioned with the state of the world around them; exploitation of the earth, wars among nations and alienation between people. They wonder why the world is this way, and how they can change it. They seek for connections between people and the earth and for more wholeness in their own lives.

The quest for stewardship of the earth is a biblical one, for God entrusted us with the dominion of the earth in Genesis 1:28. The quest for peace is also legitimate, although perfect peace on earth will not come until the return of Christ. The desire for more wholeness is similar to the Christian's desire for an integrated life of body, mind and spirit. (Although our aim is to submit all of ourselves to Christ for redemption—Rom. 12:1,2.)

All in all we must recognize that the New Age movement has some legitimate desires and is seeking answers to legitimate questions. New Age answers are wrong, but their search is not entirely evil. As Christians we must try to appeal to their questions and search. For it is in doing this, not in angry negative attacks, that the door to the gospel may be opened.

THEN, HOW DO WE RESPOND TO THE NEW AGE MOVEMENT?

So, more specifically, what can we Christians do when we encounter New Age believers or interested seekers? Based on

Douglas Groothuis's strategy in *Unmasking the New Age*, I would like to outline a three stage response.[7]

First, we must *listen* very carefully to the individuals involved to determine what they believe or what they find appealing about the New Age movement. (Since the movement is so diverse, we must be careful not to stereotype its believers.) Jesus listened to Nicodemus and also to the woman at the well before He proclaimed the gospel to them (see John 3:1-21; 4:7-26). Paul demonstrated this principle of *listening* when he carefully observed the religion of the Athenians before he began to witness to them (see Acts 17). He found out "where they were coming from." So, too, we must give our respect to people we encounter by listening to them, for they, too, are created by God and loved by Him.

> Treat each person individually, as you would want to be treated yourself. For instance, if you discover that a coworker has been through a New Age human-potential seminar, such as est, don't lecture her on its error, but engage her in conversation about her experiences and beliefs. A real and loving interest in a person's viewpoint will win more respect than a ready-made anti-New Age lecture.[8]

Second, we must *evaluate* what we have heard from the New Age believer. In evaluating, it is helpful to begin by trying to find any common points of contact between Christianity and the beliefs in question. In Acts 17 when Paul began to speak to the Athenians, he first mentioned statements of theirs that had some element of truth in them. Paul, in his observations, had found that one of the Athenian altars had an inscription, "To an Unknown God" (v. 23). Thus Paul picked up on the Athenians' belief in some sort of God. Yes, they were right to believe that there is a God, but they did not know who God really is. So Paul went on to point out the crucial differences between the Athenians' religion and the gospel (vv. 24-29).

When talking to New Age believers, we must evaluate what they tell us, both positively and negatively. First we should try to find points of agreement such as: A real belief in the spiritual side of life; or belief in some sort of God at work in the world; or a desire to change the world for the better. But then, as Paul did, we must determine the very important differences between New Age belief and Christianity. And we must be aware of our own Christian world view so that we can evaluate theirs.

Third, after having listened to and evaluated what the person has said, we must *engage* them thoughtfully. We should probe their beliefs to see what hopes and fears lie behind them so that we can communicate the gospel in a relevant way. How strongly do they hold their beliefs? Have they ever thought about Christianity and its answers to their hopes and fears? And what do they think of the Christian view of reality and its distinctions from their world view? These are all questions that can lead to a proclamation of the gospel and a proclamation that is relevant to the New Ager.

Evangelism is more than haphazardly sowing the seed of the gospel: It is translating the message of Jesus into the language of the hearer. If you can empathize with another's view of reality, then you will be able to address the needs they feel are important. When you can speak to them from their own frame of reference, it is more likely they will listen and heed your words.[9]

Again, Paul does this in his sermon in Acts 17. He finally called his hearers to repentance. "When they heard about the resurrection of the dead, some of them sneered, but others said, 'We want to hear you again on this subject.' At that, Paul left the council. A few men became followers of Paul and believed" (vv. 17:32-34).

Christians today might expect a similar response when explaining the gospel to followers of the New Age movement. Some will reject, some will want to hear more and some will believe. Those who believe will see their hopes fulfilled—not by some human effort—but by the Lord Himself when He ushers in His age of eternal, perfect peace and harmony.

Notes

1. Douglas R. Groothuis, *Confronting the New Age* (Downer Grove: InterVarsity Press, 1988), p. 19.

2. Robert J. L. Burrows, "A Vision for a New Humanity," *The New Age Rage*, ed. Karen Hoyt (Old Tappan: Revell, 1987), pp. 33-35.

3. James W. Sire, *The Universe Next Door* (Downers Grove: InterVarsity Press, 1976), p. 17.

4. Brian J. Walsh and J. Richard Middleton, *The Transforming Vision* (Downers Grove: InterVarsity Press, 1984), p. 35.

5. My descriptions of the New Age and Christian world views are based, largely, on Douglas R. Groothuis's analysis in *Unmasking the New Age* (Downers Grove: InterVarsity Press, 1986), pp. 18-31, and on Richard J. Mouw's lectures on the New Age in his course "Christian World View and Contemporary Challenges," Fuller Theological Seminary, February and March 1988.

6. Shirley MacLaine, *Out on a Limb* (New York: Bantam Books, 1983), pp. 187,188, 207-209.

7. Groothuis, *Unmasking*, pp. 174,175. See also Groothuis, *Confronting*, pp. 68-71; and Dean C. Halverson, "Spiritual Autism: Breaking Barriers by Building Bridges," *The New Age Rage*, pp. 206-210, 221-225.

8. Groothuis, *Confronting*, p. 70.

9. Halverson, "Spiritual Autism," p. 207.

8

It's a Matter of Life and Death!

ERIC PEMENT

"Which do you think is more valuable—an unborn eagle, or an unborn baby?" A pro-life group asks this question and then points to an unusual statistic:

The penalty for killing an unborn eagle in this country is a fine of up to $5000 and up to five years in prison. But killing an unborn baby is not considered a crime at all, as long as the mother approves. In fact, under certain circumstances, a doctor who does *not* advise a woman to abort her baby can be sued for hundreds of thousands of dollars.

About 4,500 unborn children are aborted in the United States every *day*. Most of these are healthy children without any mental or physical disabilities. They are simply viewed as an unwanted burden.

When tests reveal that an unborn child is imperfect, many people who would not consider abortion under normal circumstances, choose to have the baby aborted. The possibility of raising a disabled child is frightening to many parents. So much so that Dr. Francis Crick and Dr. James Watson, who won the Nobel prize for discovering DNA, have recommended that a baby not be declared "fully human" until three days after the baby's birth, so that the parents might legally destroy it if it appears defective. Although this suggestion seems logical to some scientists, it outrages others.

LIFE: A VERY TOUCHY SUBJECT

Why are people so touchy when it comes to abortion? I've seen good friends and family members, who like to gab about anything and everything, refuse to discuss abortion for fear of having an argument. Abortion is a supersensitive matter because it strikes at the heart of what it means to be human. If the fetus isn't really human, then killing it is no more significant than killing a chicken or a puppy. But if the unborn child *is* human, then killing him is murder.

The same uneasy feelings pop up when people are asked hard questions about infanticide (the killing of infants) and euthanasia ("mercy killing"). Often euthanasia and infanticide are not considered to be in the same category as abortion since in most Western cultures abortion is legal and euthanasia and infanticide are not. However, the moral questions are very similar, and the point at which letting a person die becomes euthanasia or infanticide is not always clear.

In a famous case, parents in Indiana decided to allow their baby, known to thousands of Americans as "Baby Doe," to starve to death rather than letting the child have a routine surgical procedure to unblock his esophagus. The parents' reason? The baby had Down's syndrome, a genetic disorder that causes mental retardation. The Indiana Supreme Court sanctioned the parents' decision.[1] Was this legal action morally wrong?

Relatives may contemplate "mercy killing" of an adult who is terminally ill or who may be permanently comatose though still alive. Many times the families of these patients ask doctors to stop heroic measures to save the patient. To most, this is simply allowing a natural death to occur. But when feeding tubes are withdrawn or food and water withheld, the question must be asked, is this a natural death or euthanasia?

One day you may have to decide whether to withhold life support systems for a family member or allow surgery to save a severely handicapped, premature infant. Any decision like this demands careful reasoning and the ability to see through faulty arguments. Thinking through the moral, ethical and spiritual implications ahead of time will help you make a better decision should such a crisis arise. If you do not think through the issues, you may rely solely upon the judgment of the medical professionals who are with you at the time. Just because a person is a doctor doesn't mean he or she can reach the right conclusions or shares your values. If a person starts with the wrong assumptions about life, he or she will end up with the wrong conclusions or decisions.

Any decision Christians come to about the sanctity of life should not be determined by cultural standards. Whether "most people" agree or disagree on the sanctity of life is not important. In the final analysis we should be led by the written Word of God, prayer, medical evidence and careful reason. The basic issue for Christians is not is human life sacred? Christians would agree that as God's image-bearers, it is. The question is, how do my beliefs, attitudes and actions support the sanctity of life?

WHY TAKE INNOCENT LIFE?

The reasons people support abortion, infanticide and euthanasia are far more numerous than we could list here. Scores of books have been written on the subject. But most of the arguments revolve around two main points:

1. The first is usually called "quality of life." It says, how can it be worth living if you're severely crippled? If a child or an adult becomes so profoundly retarded that he doesn't even know his own name, the person isn't fully human. For one family to face the medical expenses of caring for such a person, is just too much. Also even if society could afford the high costs, suppose the baby's mother didn't want him or love him? It would be better for all concerned if the child were aborted or dead. Joseph Fletcher, best known for defending "situation ethics," believes a patient's "personhood" should be evaluated in light of "perceived quality of life" (his term) rather than on the biological fact of life.

The basic issue for Christians is not is human life sacred? Christians would agree that as God's image-bearers, it is. The question is, how do my beliefs, attitudes and actions support the sanctity of life?

This concept is widely accepted in society, but stands in contrast to the traditional Christian principle asserting the sanctity of all human life regardless of its quality.[2]

2. The second main point, that usually applies to abortion, is "freedom of choice." It says the choice to bear a child or to abort should be left up to the mother.

This idea is expressed in a number of ways: "Well, abortion isn't anything for anybody to pass judgment on but me." "A woman should have the right to control her own body and determine her own future." "It's my body, it's my life." "If you don't believe in abortion, you don't have to have one, but don't tell me *I* can't have one."

If you examine these statements carefully, you'll see they are different ways of arguing for freedom of choice. Sometimes these arguments for abortion can sound awfully convincing. This is especially true in Western cultures such as that of the United States where self-determination is given near-sacred status. Preserving free choice in such issues may be equated with preserving democracy. But Carl F. H. Henry, founding editor of *Christianity Today* and lecturer-at-large for World Vision International, sees the idea that "democracy is secure as long as individual's rights are stressed" as one of the common fallacies of Western thought. He states, "Without shared values, democracy is on the move to anarchy."[3] Addressing the issue of choice as it relates to abortion, Henry proposes, "Abortion cannot be catalogued with suicide as a merely personal decision, since the life involved is not the mother's own."[4]

STEPS ON THE LADDER OF LOGIC

To judge abortion, infanticide, euthanasia and bio-medical technological practices wisely, we must approach it by examining the fundamentals. In fact, this method should be used when you're trying to understand any difficult subject, not just those mentioned above.

First, consider the basic values, the fundamental issues at stake. What's at the heart of the matter? Question the *principles*, not the program. Next, determine which values or principles should take priority over other values. (One sure way of knowing which principles are more important is by studying what the Bible says.) Look at the exceptions last.

Although exceptions may occur, an exception—a rare, one-in-a-million case—should never force you to toss out a rule that is good 99 percent of the time. Likewise, a fact that is questionable or trivial should never be used to overthrow or "cross out" a fact that is solidly proven and well-established. (For example: Just because scientists can't figure out how the honeybee is able to fly, doesn't make all of aeronautics worthless.)

We'll use the step-by-step method in dealing with the sanctity of life. We begin with the foundational question of human beings—why are people important? The answer to this question will set the stage. The next step is to examine the unborn fetus and the comatose or severely afflicted person. Are they alive? Are they human? Are they significant? Finally, we'll talk about the "hard cases": When might it be permissible to take away the life of an unborn child? When might it be permissible to withhold medical treatment from a child or adult?

WHAT ARE PEOPLE REALLY WORTH?

If life came about by a chance accident, and human beings are nothing more than two-legged mobile "computers" using carbon cells instead of silicon chips, then why shouldn't we treat people like machines? Machines have no "rights"—we can chop them up, sell them or we can destroy them if they fail to live up to our desires.

However, human beings possess a wholly different character than anything else on earth. Not just because we are alive; plants are alive. Not just because we can think; chimpanzees and gorillas can think.

Humans are unique because we were created by God and bear God's image. From the Einstein to the drunk in the gutter, each person carries a spiritual nature that comes from God—a soul, a character that bears the imprint of the Creator. In Genesis 1:27 we find that God created humankind, both male and female, in His own image. This "image" was not erased by Adam and Eve; according to James, we still retain God's "likeness" (Jas. 3:9).

To most of the world, people's importance depends on who they know, what they can do and how much they possess. But in the eyes of God, each person is of enormous importance. God does not value us because of our looks, our strength, our I.Q. or our money; He loves each person individually. Each person is unique and has value, even if that person is "unwanted" by his friends or "unloved" by her mother. Jesus Christ loves that person regardless.

Each person has a right to life, even if he or she can't "contribute" to society. Jesus identified Himself with the outcast, not with the in-crowd, when He said, "Whatever you did for one of the *least* of these brothers of mine, you did for me" (Matt. 25:40, emphasis added). God is no respecter of persons—He does not play favorites (Acts 10:34; Eph. 6:9)—and His regard for people is not based on their social or intellectual capacities.

WHAT IS THE UNBORN CHILD?

Although some people can look at this question and say, "Easy answer!" other people have difficulty with it. For some people the unborn child is just "fetal tissue" or a "product of conception." The implication of such language is that the unborn baby is something less than human.

A few people dislike calling the fetus a "baby" because they don't believe the fetus is a human life yet. Even the U. S. Supreme Court in its famous 1973 abortion decision (Roe v. Wade) said that it couldn't resolve "the difficult question of when human life begins."

However, medical doctors, biology teachers and even most abortionists admit that life of some sort begins at conception. Indeed, 10 years before the Supreme Court's abortion decision, Planned Parenthood distributed a pamphlet that stated an abortion kills the life of a baby after it has begun.

This can be seen fairly easily.

The same standards for life used for plants and animals at any level of complexity can be used to show that a fertilized egg or a developing fetus do, indeed, qualify as "life." The difference between a dead body and a live one is not whether it has DNA or is made up of cells, but whether it carries out certain biological functions. These basic life functions would include consumption of food, metabolism, respiration, elimination of waste, growth and movement, and the capacity to reproduce when the organism reaches maturity. This is how biologists and most dictionaries define "life."

You don't have to be a biochemist to recognize that the human embryo carries on all the functions of life from the moment of conception. A simple thing to remember is that if the fetus weren't alive, it wouldn't grow and move.

Is the fetus a human life?

Well, it's certainly not *plant* life! And I don't know too many people who would claim it's a form of bird or reptile life.

Even if the fact that the fetus is living were not obvious, the possibility that it is living should be enough to warrant protection. Ronald Reagan stated this argument very practically when he said, "If you don't know whether a body is alive or dead, you would never bury it. I think this consideration itself should be enough for all of us to insist on protecting the unborn."[5]

We all know the unborn child is not fully grown and is immature. But the humanity of an unborn baby can never be doubted, just as the "birdness" of an unborn eagle should never be doubted.

"If you don't know whether a body is alive or dead, you would never bury it. I think this consideration itself should be enough for all of us to insist on protecting the unborn."[5]

But there's more. Biological evidences for the humanity of the unborn child, however true they may be, still do not convey the whole story.

The Scripture gives the view that can never be seen by biology and medicine. In it, God reveals that He has a plan for each person's life, and that He is involved in our growth and development from the very beginning.

In the book of Psalms, King David describes his creation by God: "For you created my inmost being; you knit me together in my mother's womb. I praise you because I am fearfully and wonderfully made; your works are wonderful, I know that full well. My frame was not hidden from you when I was made in the secret place. When I was woven together in the depths of the earth, your eyes saw my unformed body. All the days ordained for me were written in your book before one of them came to be" (Ps. 139:13-16).

Seen in this light the unborn child is not merely a developing human organism (though the baby *is* that, of course). God declares that He has also ordained a purpose and a course of life for that child, standing behind the child's formation in the womb long before the child is born.

Now, after looking at the Bible's estimate of human life, and especially the value of unborn children, we can examine the main arguments for abortion, infanticide and euthanasia in their proper perspective.

WHEN SHOULD LIFE BE TAKEN AWAY?

One final tip on clear thinking: Don't let anyone snow you into thinking that because something is *legal*, then it must be *right*. The two are not the same. It's legal in many countries to be a drunk, a pornographer, a racist and a Satanist. In Nazi Germany, it was legal to kill Jews. However, just because something is permissible under national law doesn't mean it's acceptable in the eyes of God.

Now, what about abortion, infanticide and euthanasia?

If humans are made in God's image, and life is a special gift given to us by God, and if unborn children are truly human, then the basic idea of abortion is wrong for the same reason murder is wrong. God gives life to humans, and He forbids the murder of innocent people (see Deut. 27:25). If we have no right to kill people simply because they are ugly, poor, or of the "wrong" color or language, then how can we justify killing people because they inconvenience us financially or do not meet our standards for intelligence?

If the life of a helpless fetus is forfeitable . . . do the mother and father, in principle, forfeit any right to their own survival if they become helpless and their children are disposed to destroy them?[6] Most people would answer no. Yet when the sacredness of human life in the form of the unborn is undermined, the sanctity of all humanity is diminished.

I have seen severely deformed children who would be considered "basket cases" by some people. It is their *humanity* that gives them value, not their marketable skills or their "quality of life." People have intrinsic value simply because they are human, regardless of what they may be capable of by earthly standards.

To cause the death of a person suffering from an illness, severe handicap or senility is to interfere with God's providence. As Christian ethicist Paul Ramsey puts it, "To choose to assist the dying process actively is to throw the gift of life back in the face of the Giver."[7]

But what about freedom of choice?

Certainly, we know that both men and women have a right to freedom of choice. The United States Declaration of Independence put it this way: That among the rights God has given man are the right to "life, liberty, and the pursuit of happiness." To a certain extent, this right to liberty includes freedom of speech, of religion, of assembly, of occupation and of things that pertain to a person's future.

However, the right to personal liberty has limits. We cannot shout "fire" in a crowded theater, we cannot assemble to overthrow the government, and we may not exercise our rights in a way that endangers or restricts someone else's rights. In short, there is a priority of rights, that is summed up in this maxim: "Your rights end where my nose begins."

One of the arguments for "choice" in having an abortion is that a woman has a right to control her own body. To a certain degree, this is true. However, the unborn child is not just an attachment to the woman's body. The unborn child has his *own* body, with his own DNA (quite different from the mother's), his own fingerprints (visible at three months), and his own independent heart and bloodstream. Often, even the blood type is different! So while a woman may have the right to her own life and liberty, that doesn't give her the right to take away her child's life.

An objection that comes up quite often is, "You may not believe in abortion, but at least give the mother the freedom to decide for herself." But in the case of abortion, what this is asking for is the choice to save or kill an unborn baby. Under the normal course of law, we do not give a person the choice to kill innocent people. Maybe this illustration will help.

In the United States 150 years ago, slavery was acceptable in some states and the black slave was not considered a true "person." The Southern states argued that each state should be free to choose for itself whether to permit slavery. They told the North, "If you don't believe in slavery, you can outlaw slavery in your state. But don't impose your values on us."

The United States eventually reached the breaking point on this issue, culminating in the Civil War. Although our national conscience was dim for years on the subject of slavery, it was eventually provoked to see that human rights superseded financial benefit. No doubt the slaveholders supposed that their "majority vote" gave them a right to own slaves. Unfortunately, this interpretation of "choice" took away the life and liberty of millions of human beings.

Abraham Lincoln warned against devaluing the lives of any human beings: "I should like to know if taking this old Declaration of Independence, which declares that all men are equal upon principle, and making exceptions to it, where will it stop? If one man says it does not mean a Negro, why not another say it does not mean some other man?"[8]

One of the final problems of the "freedom of choice" argument as it applies to abortion is that it sees only two possibilities. Either abort, or be stuck with a baby the rest of your life. This is not true; there are more than two options. The mother could give the baby up for adoption, which would seem to be far more humane than aborting him.

WHAT ABOUT THE HARD CASES?

Would abortion be acceptable following a case of rape?

As evil and as hateful as rape is, killing the innocent party is not the answer. The baby was not guilty of any crime. The child's conception may have come about through an evil act, but the child himself is not evil and has the same potential for good as any human being. In the rare instance where bearing a baby normally would endanger the health of the mother (sometimes a rape victim is young), special medical treatment to preserve both mother and child should be sought.

A very hard decision must be made when a pregnancy would literally kill the mother. For example, such a case might be an ectopic (or "tubal") pregnancy, or perhaps the discovery of uterine cancer, where an immediate hysterectomy is needed. If the baby continues to grow, both mother and child will die.

On such occasions when faced with two certain deaths (unless God miraculously intervenes), it seems to me the only alternative is to abort the child. An innocent life is still taken, however, and we should seek to save the child if at all possible.

The *ideal* solution would be to move a tubally-implanted fetus to a safe location within the uterus. Currently, we cannot move the fetus without killing it, but as medical technology advances, this may become possible.

With the advancement of medical technology, many new questions are arising that Christians must confront:

● Since abortions are already occurring, should scientists be allowed to use aborted fetal tissue in experiments or in medical treatments?

● Since some people will their bodies to science, does a mother have the right to donate her aborted fetus to science?

● Is it wrong to take a very premature, severely handicapped newborn off life support systems? If no, does that include nutrition and hydration tubes? If your response to the second question is yes, would it be kinder to give the child a lethal injection rather than allowing him to die slowly of starvation?

● At what point should a family refuse heroic medical procedures to save a terminal or senile family member? Or, should everything possible always be done to save a life, no matter what the condition of the patient?

● Is keeping a comatose person, with no electrical brain activity, on life support systems the same as trapping his soul in his body?

● Is it morally proper for doctors to recommend abortion? If yes, under what circumstances?

● Is it alright for a Christian to refuse chemotherapy? If his or her prognosis would be improved with chemotherapy, is refusing it the same as suicide?

● Is it acceptable to harvest organs from a comatose or brain dead patient?

The answers to some of these questions may be more obvious than others. And almost certainly, advances in science and technology will raise new questions in the near future.

CONSISTENCY AND COMPASSION

To sum up then, a consistent view of abortion, infanticide and mercy killing is one that begins from the most basic platform—

the value of human beings. Then, with compassion we try to work out the best way to solve human problems, while safeguarding human life.

Sometimes two things will come into conflict, such as a woman's right to be free from the cost and burden of pregnancy, and the child's right to live. Obviously, if a wife is unprepared or unwilling to become a mother, the time to make that decision is before the baby is conceived. She and her husband should take steps to prevent conception.

In the same light, if a woman is unmarried, if she would follow the Bible's instruction to "flee from sexual immorality" (1 Cor. 6:18) and remain sexually pure, most of the problems of unwanted pregnancy (and most of the reasons for abortion) would be solved. This does not let the men off the hook, though the problem of abortion is a national sin and the male's responsibility for this sin is at *least* equal to the woman's, if not greater.

When people have fallen into sexual sin and a child has been conceived in the process, the answer is not to tell the mother to escape the consequences of the sin by killing the child, thus committing a greater sin. The Christian response is to respect the new life that has been created, recognize that the child has as much a right to live as any of us do and do what we can to aid both mother and child in building a new life.

Likewise, the Christian response to the handicapped, very ill and very old is to love them and respect them. Those caring for afflicted family members should be supported by the family of believers. The appropriateness of using modern bio-medical technology should be evaluated carefully. But actively participating in bringing on death should be considered inappropriate for Christians.

Science has expanded human convenience and comfort. But it has not made humanity wiser, better or happier. And science is not in the position to evaluate the moral implication of some of its achievements. Christian people need to involve themselves in the evaluation process. It is a part of the duty of the Church in its function of being salt and light in a shadowy, dark world.

Notes

1. President Ronald W. Reagan, *Abortion and the Conscience of the Nation* (Washington, D.C.: Government Printing Office, 1983), pp. 3,4.
2. Ed Larson and Beth Spring, "Life-defying Acts," *Christianity Today* (March 6, 1987), p.19.
3. Carl F. H. Henry, *Christian Countermoves in a Decadent Culture* (Portland: Multnomah Press, 1986), p. 31.
4. Ibid, p. 59.
5. Reagan, *Abortion and the Conscience of the Nation*, p. 3.
6. Henry, *Christian Countermoves*, p. 59.
7. Larson and Spring, "Life-defying Acts," p. 19.
8. Reagan, *Abortion and the Conscience of the Nation*, p. 6.

Pro-life: More than Just a Catchy Term _____

Right-to-lifers are sometimes citicized for not being pro-*life*, but only pro-*fetal* life. Critics argue that the life of the potential mother is often dismissed lightly in the concern over the unborn. Unfortunately, there is some truth to this complaint. Women seeking abortions may be stereotyped as calloused murderers who can't put up with a little inconvenience. In reality, these women or girls are often victims themselves—of rape, incest, naivete, poverty, neglectful parents, abandonment, condemnation or social pressure. Christians need to keep in mind that there is more than one victim involved in abortion, and God loves both equally. To save the unborn the potential mother must be reached. Here are some constructive ways to minister to these girls or women in order to counteract abortion:

Community Support Groups
Often the potential mother feels she is alone with the problem of her pregnancy. We are to bear one another's burdens to fulfill the law of Christ (see Gal. 6:2). We can help her bear her burdens through:
- Counseling centers
- Developing surrogate extended family support
- Homes for unwed mothers
- Child development classes
- Crisis hotlines

Legislation or Fundraising
A deciding factor for abortion is often the financial burden of bearing and caring for children. By becoming informed of pending legislation and by fundraising for private organizations, Christians can help provide:
- Day Care Centers
- Assistance during maternity leave
- Nutrition and education aid for poor children
- Financial help for parents of the handicapped

Compassion
Consider that in a recent survey "61 percent of the teenage mothers reported they were sexually abused as children" (Administered by the Illinois Department of Children and Family Services, *Youthworker Update*, November 1987, pp. 3,4). A pregnant teen does not simply mean an immoral teen. A woman considering abortion does not necessarily equal a casual killer. These are people who have often been badly hurt and need someone's compassion in order to heal and in order to make good decisions in the future.

Tragically, the judgment by people of women who become

pregnant outside of marriage may be the cause of many abortions. In a 1987 survey of 1,900 women who had abortions, a third of the women said that they had abortions because they didn't want other people to know they were pregnant (Joyce Price, "Catholic Abortions Rate Highest of All Faiths," *Washington Times*, October 7, 1988, Section A, p. 7). If women feel their behavior is unacceptable/unforgiveable, they may add to that unacceptable behavior the act of abortion. Compassion for the potential mother is not only crucial for her well-being, but leads to better care for the unborn.

Pro-life vs. Anti-abortion

If we are to take the word seriously, being pro-life does not stop at concern that a fetus will come to full term. There are people all over the world who have made it through birth and yet face death daily because of neglect. They are as much our responsibility as the unborn. People who need our help include:

- The poverty-stricken in third-world countries (comprising two thirds of the world's countries)
- Children in abusive homes
- The elderly on fixed or no incomes
- People imprisoned under inhumane conditions
- The homeless (There are 3 million homeless in the United States. An estimated 30 percent of those are children [National Coalition for the Homeless, 1988].)

The list could go on, but the message is clear. If we are to use the slogan, "Pro-life," we must respond to its *full* meaning.

By Judith L. Roth

9

I Was Young, But . . .

RUTH M. BATHAUER

"I don't intend to grow old gracefully. I intend to fight it each step of the way!" Have you seen the TV commercial for Oil of Olay in which a beautiful woman declares her fight against old age? Most of us are quick to identify with her and to jump on her bandwagon. We jog, diet, color our hair and invest in cosmetics in our attempt to halt the aging process. And cosmetic surgery has become a popular vehicle to prevent aging with many adults. Despite our best efforts, however, the clock ticks on without mercy shoving each of us until we reach the senior adult age bracket of 56 and up.

It's not so difficult to notice that friends and relatives are aging, but to discover the first gray hair or wrinkle facing you in the mirror can be traumatic.

It can also be a shock when we meet people we've not seen in years. In our minds they continue in the blush of youth. But reality may be far different.

A friend flew back east for her twenty-fifth high school reunion recently. When questioned, it was obvious she was slightly disappointed in seeing her peers. "All we saw," she said, "were senior citizens!"

It is estimated that by 1990 there will be about 50,000 centenarians, and according to statistics from the Metropolitan Life Insurance Company this huge number will jump to 100,000 by the year 2000. The U.S. Census Bureau reports that there are nearly 7 million Americans over the age of 80 at the present time.

Whether we like it or not, if we continue to live each of us will eventually face the 56-year-old plus mark. People have different reactions to the aging process despite the fact that everyone ages at exactly the same rate—one day at a time. Most would like to ignore aging. Some fight it, but there comes a time to face reality. The aging process begins the moment we are born. So, whether you are now a senior adult or much younger, one day you will face aging and its problems.

Although the popular belief is that old age is something of a curse, God never intended that. The Bible also gives specific guidelines concerning our attitudes toward the elderly: "Rise in the presence of the aged, show respect for the elderly and revere your God" (Lev. 19:32). And "Do not despise your mother when she is old" (Prov. 23:22). With due respect to hair tints, I like Proverbs 16:31, "Gray hair is a crown of splendor; it is attained by a righteous life."

These exhortations continue in the New Testament (see Eph. 6:2,3; 1 Tim. 5:4). According to God's Word, young and old are accountable for one another.

The English poet, Robert Browning, wrote at age 52:

"Grow old along with me! The best is yet to be, The last of

life, for which the first was made! Our times are in His hand."[1]

If we agree that our times are in God's hand and if we keep the teaching of His Word in proper perspective, we will be able to deal with the aging process.

A TIME FOR EVERYTHING

King Solomon, a very wise man said, "There is a time for everything, and a season for every activity under heaven" (Eccles. 3:1). For the senior adult it is time to consider several areas of life.

A Time for Fitness

It is fashionable to be on a health kick, to eat the right food and to keep fit and trim. Because our bodies are so visible, it is disconcerting to face the reality of slight weakening in muscle tone or other obvious decline. On the heels of that discovery comes problems with bodily functions and the haunting feeling of possible immobility or even helplessness.

If you are now a couch potato and your exercise consists of moving from your desk to the dinner table to the den where you're glued to the TV tube all evening, you are asking for trouble.

While we must face aging, there is no need to panic at the first indication of decreasing energy. Begin a systematic routine to keep your body strong. If you are now a couch potato and your exercise consists of moving from your desk to the dinner table to the den where you're glued to the TV tube all evening, you are asking for trouble. Get out of your easy chair, and take a walk. Go swimming or ride a bike. A body that is active won't rust and stiffen.

It is wise to check with your doctor first to get a sensible exercise routine. In discussing a diet and exercise routine with him or her, you will find there is a definite emphasis on the healthy senior adult. New discoveries and advancements in science, medicine and nutrition have extended our life span to new limits. The U.S. Census Bureau indicates that in 1986 life expectancy reached a record of 78.9 for white females and 72 for white males; 73.6 years for black females and 65.5 years for black males.[2] As born-again believers our bodies are the temples of the Holy Spirit. It seems to me that we need to do all we can to keep our temples in good repair. A half hour of exercise each day can do wonders to make you feel young and strong—even at age 56 plus.

A Time for Financial Assessment

This is not a chapter on finances, but with soaring prices who among us, regardless of age, does not feel concerned about the future? As a senior adult this is a time to move carefully when considering high-risk investments because there isn't enough time to earn and regain mammoth losses.

If you are one who has left all financial matters to your spouse, now is the time for a change—nothing drastic—just a careful plan. While you are both together, it is important that you become familiar with your financial status so that when the time comes when your spouse is no longer with you, you will know what to do. If you have been the financial manager, you need to acquaint your spouse with such matters as budget, debts, mortgages, investments, insurances, pensions and your will. One should not have the overwhelming confusion and fear of unknown financial how-to added to the grief of the loss of a spouse. Many financial consultants advise senior adults to plan ahead and arrange for a power of attorney to take effect if and when they become infirmed.

No one likes to think of nursing care, but too often that care becomes a necessity. The cost for extended care in a nursing home is estimated to be from $20 to $30 thousand a year and rising. Unfortunately, at this time Medicare does not pay for extended care. Investigate insurance policies available to help cover the cost. The sooner you buy the policy the lower the premiums.

Suppose there are no pensions, no stocks or bonds, only a small fixed income? It is still smart to plan and to be a good steward of your finances, especially when we see our resources slipping away not only on a national but also on a worldwide scale. We can't deny that good stewardship is a must.

It is wise to investigate now what agencies are available should you find yourself faced with living on a small fixed income. By calling the Family Service or Welfare Department, you can find out where and how food stamps can be secured. Investigate available Social Security supplements. In other words, good stewardship requires that you do as much as you can by careful planning. Although Christians have differing viewpoints on receiving government assistance, they would agree that whatever the means, God is their ultimate security and source. Never forget that as a Christian you belong to the Lord who promised to supply *all* your needs (see Phil. 4:19).

A Time to Face Retirement

Retirement is a major concern for senior adults. Sure, you've planned and dreamed of what you would do when the time finally comes. But many people who are within a year or two of actual retirement confess that they are not ready for it.

People hate change. We like things the way they are. The retiree often feels he will lose his identity with retirement because we tend to identify ourselves by our careers. We're teachers, lawyers, bookkeepers. How does one maintain his or her identify after retirement? The good news is that born-again believers, whether retired or not, are and always will be "heirs of God and co-heirs with Christ" (Rom. 8:17). Who can ask for a better I.D.?

While we may feel insecure without our work schedules, God gives us the ability to adjust to the changes. Elizabeth Skoglund, a family counselor, says that one of the best ways to avoid the fearful potential infirmity of old age is to become steeped in the Bible.[3] God's message can also do wonders to change a depressed attitude that often comes with retirement.

Retirement and old age must be accepted. Naturally, there will be changes as we give up some things and take on others that we may not like. Preparation for retirement, however, makes the changes easier. Begin now to prepare mentally and emotionally for retirement. Try to get a clear concept of what changes you will face. What problems will the changes bring? How will you solve these problems? What resources can you use to help you?

Retirement doesn't mean that a worthwhile, purposeful life comes to a screeching halt. More free time should be a challenge for continued growth and development.

Dr. Lloyd H. Ahlem, director of the Covenant Village Retirement Center, Turlock, California, suggests that you visualize a typical day's activity in the early weeks of retirement. Your plan for the first days of retirement should not be very different from your last days of work, says Dr. Ahlem. If you laze about, sleep late, watch hours of TV, you'll soon feel bored and out of sorts. Lack of mental and physical activity will create health problems.

FEARS TO HAUNT SENIOR ADULTS

As the long shadows of aging fall on the life of the senior adult, there are certain fears that raise their ugly heads. We need to face our fears and realize that some, within reason, are normal. If a person's eyesight is failing or he's had one heart attack, he has a right to wonder how he will manage alone. Other fears, however, are myths and some result from the unhealthy attitude that constantly asks, "Why does this happen to me?"

While we cannot list all of the fears that come with aging, let's look at a few of the typical ones.

Fear of Loneliness

The person who sees friends, relatives or a spouse pass away faces real feelings of loneliness. When my father died, I was ready to move from Chicago to California to be with my elderly mother. I dreaded the loneliness she faced in her empty home. But my mother, the eternal optimist, had a deep faith in God. When I suggested my idea she said, "I appreciate your love and concern, but you can never take Dad's place. I am no different from others in this world—with His help I will find my place."

And she did. Several widowed ladies in her church became not only a support group for each other, but also fast friends. On Sundays they often went to a little coffee shop for dinner. It was within walking distance and the price fit fixed budgets.

Loneliness is an empty space that needs to be filled. Eighty-year-old Beulah managed to avoid loneliness by writing letters. She wrote not only to her friends but to missionaries, shut-ins and to young people away at college assuring them of her prayers. Her favorite gift was to receive a small check that she immediately exchanged for stationery and stamps.

Fear of Environmental Change

Ours is a mobile society. Friends and children move away for new jobs or other reasons. Neighborhoods change and become unsafe. The time may come when poor health dictates that you can no longer live alone. Giving up the home filled with fond memories is hard. Many senior adults lash out in fear, frustration and anger at their children when they, in love, suggest a change.

Long before the time comes for a move, pray about it and your attitude. Don't lay a guilt trip on your children by blaming them for the change. Talk to them, even though it is difficult, and honestly express your fears of moving. Then pray with your children and believe God will guide both them and you.

Warren and Betty made an agreement with their father not to sell or rent out his home while he tried living in a retirement center. If, after two months, he decided it didn't work out, he could go back home and they would consider other supervised living arrangements. The Lord answered prayer. Although the first few weeks were rough, the father eventually found new friends and real contentment in the center.

The Fear of Senility

There is a myth that it is impossible to learn after a certain age. That concept is just that—a myth. Educators have proven that learning never ceases. The learning process may slow down a bit, but the learning ability goes on. Experts, working with the elderly, urge seniors to pursue mental activities: read, stay mentally alert, work crossword puzzles.

Instead of worrying about losing your mind, check out the courses offered through adult education in your area. You'll find courses in everything from cake decorating to photography to archaeology. Just for the fun of it, broaden your thinking by taking a course in a subject you've never had time to explore. Just think how much you will be able to stimulate a conversation and impress your friends!

Fear of Immobility

The loss of health resulting in confinement is a great fear. David B. Oliver, Ph.D., while speaking at the 1981 Conference on Aging said that our society has overemphasized the concept of the fragile and disabled elderly. According to statistics, poor health has limited only 16 percent of senior adults. But, Dr. Oliver indicated that 84 percent are enjoying fairly healthy lives.[4] These facts are encouraging. We hear many negative comments concerning the fate of the elderly, but for the Christian there is always hope. We belong to a great God. Troubles will come, of course, but He will not forsake His own (see Heb. 13:5).

Fear of Not Being Needed

Inner needs do not change as people advance in years. Humans always have a need for identity, acceptance, fulfillment and love no matter what their age. One way many fulfill this need is knowing that they have a place in their families. So to people advancing in years a haunting fear is the question: What if my family should no longer need me?

Maude was a sparkling, friendly widow whom I first met when she was in her 70s. Although her family lived far away, it was evident Maude *created* a place for herself by her attitude and her seemingly innate ability to help others.

Very active in her church, Maude encouraged many of her peers by visiting convalescent hospitals and shut-ins. She still drove her car and often provided transportation to meetings, outings and other functions. Instead of waiting to be needed, Maude looked for needs to be filled and thereby she exuded warmth and cheer wherever she went.

ANTIDOTE FOR FEARS

God's Word offers an antidote for fear. The Lord promises His presence in the most difficult situations (see Isa. 43:1,2). And the psalmist verifies that promise: "I was young and now I am old, yet I have never seen the righteous forsaken" (Ps. 37:25). As an older man the psalmist has had vast experiences and opportunity for extended observation. His conclusion is that God protects and blesses His people. The joys, hopes and vigor of youth are gone—"I *was* young." Now the psalmist can vouch for the fact that God does not forsake His own. He never promised a trouble-free life, but God is faithful and is with us *in* trouble.

THE BEST IS YET TO BE

Do you believe that "the best is yet to be" despite problems that may arise? I do. Elijah had a great spiritual experience on Mount Carmel when God demonstrated His power in a spectacular way. When fire fell in answer to Elijah's simple prayer in the contest between Baal and the living God, the amazed crowd could only declare, "The Lord—he is God!" (1 Kings 18:39). Then came the let-down, and Elijah wanted to die. He was worn out, fearful and depressed. Ready to give up he wailed, "I am the only one left" (1 Kings 19:10).

Often senior adults have a tendency to echo Elijah's cry. Notice God didn't reprimand His prophet. The Lord did, however, shake Elijah out of the doldrums. There was work to be done! After giving Elijah several assignments (vv. 15-17), God added a gentle reminder when He said in effect, "Elijah, you're not alone—there are still seven thousand left who follow me" (v. 18).

As a senior adult when you feel depressed and lonely, remember that there is still work for you. And you're not alone! There are almost 7 million who are over the age of 80 in the United States alone.

Prayer
No matter what your physical condition, you can pray. At retirement you have more time than ever before. Look at needs around you and then make a prayer list. Keep a journal and date your requests and God's answers. That means, of course, you must believe that God keeps His promises. And He does (see Num.

23:19)—not always the way we expect, but He answers. You will find your faith growing as you experience the excitement of answered prayer.

Share Your Experience

You have a lifetime of experiences and ability to share. If, for example, you are a retired teacher, you could visit the local school board or teachers association and offer to become a tutor for slow learners. Many adults today are unable to read. Does your community have a reading program for illiterate adults who would benefit from your ability?

Day care centers offer another opportunity. These centers are often looking for assistance from people who are willing to become adoptive grandparents to lonely children.

If you have walked with the Lord for many years, don't let the wealth of knowledge become dormant.

Oliver is a skilled artist who worked for years as a commercial engraver. Many art schools no longer teach that skill, therefore a number of young artists have benefited from Oliver's willingness to teach them the skill.

Share Your Wisdom

If you have walked with the Lord for many years, don't let the wealth of knowledge become dormant. Contact your church and offer to teach a Bible class. Or invite other people in your neighborhood to have a time of fellowship and Bible study in your home. Like the psalmist, tell of your observations of God's blessing and faithfulness. You can offer living proof of what He can and has done.

Conclusion

There is no limit to the contribution you as a senior adult can make to society if you ask the Lord for guidance and make yourself available. God's commands and promises remain the same regardless of your age, because He does not change (see Heb. 13:8). His Word challenges senior adults to teach the younger generation (see Titus 2:2-6). And with that challenge comes a blessed promise: "The righteous will flourish . . . . They *will still bear fruit in old age* . . . proclaiming, 'The Lord is upright; he is my Rock'" (Ps. 92:12-15, emphasis added).

Notes

1. Robert Browning, "Rabbi Ben Ezra," 1864, Public domain.
2. Tad Szulc, "How Can We Help Ourselves Age with Dignity," *Star Free Press, Parade Magazine*, May 29, 1988, p. 6.
3. Elizabeth Skoglund, *A Divine Blessing* (Minneapolis: World Wide Publications, 1988).
4. David B. Oliver, Ph.D. *Ministering to the Aged* (Pomona, CA: Focus on the Family, 1984).

There Is a Season ———————————————

In an age where youth is beauty and the strength and energy of youth are revered, it is sometimes difficult for adults to accept that they are growing older. Difficult to accept that each day takes them farther from their youth. This loss of youth is accompanied by other losses as well, as each phase of life passes:

- the carefree irresponsibility before marriage and a family;
- the irretrievable sweet time when the children are babies;
- the feeling of usefulness as you carry out your role of breadwinner and/or parent;

- the sense of security that often is there when your parents are alive and capable.

Each change brings loss. But change also brings an opportunity for gain:

- with the "empty nest," your spouse and your house are your own again;
- your baby girl will grow up, but she might bless you with grandchildren;
- with retirement comes the chance to do all those things you never had time for before;
- you might not look as pert as you did at 19, but would you want to trade all that you've learned as you matured just to be youthful again?

As the Teacher of Ecclesiastes said, "There is a time for everything, and a season for every activity under heaven" (Eccles. 3:1). Treasure the memories of the wonderful things in the past and eagerly look forward to the glorious things of the present and future.

By Judith L. Roth

10

Church and State

DAVID EDWARDS

Should Christians obey the law and the instructions of government authorities? Take your time before answering; there's more to this question than you might think.

THE QUESTION:
MUST WE ALWAYS OBEY THE GOVERNMENT?

What Paul Says in Romans 13
In the thirteenth chapter of his Epistle to the Romans, Paul makes statements about our Christian duty to obey the government. For nearly 2,000 years these statements have caused great confusion and debate among Christians:

> Everyone must submit himself to the governing authorities, for there is no authority except that which God has

established. The authorities that exist have been established by God. Consequently, he who rebels against the authority is rebelling against what God has instituted, and those who do so will bring judgment on themselves. For rulers hold no terror for those who do right, but for those who do wrong. Do you want to be free from fear of the one in authority? Then do what is right and he will commend you. For he is God's servant to do you good. But if you do wrong, be afraid, for he does not bear the sword for nothing. He is God's servant, an agent of wrath to bring punishment on the wrongdoer. Therefore, it is necessary to submit to the authorities, not only because of possible punishment but also because of conscience. This is also why you pay taxes, for the authorities are God's servants, who give their full time to governing. Give everyone what you owe him: If you owe taxes, pay taxes; if revenue, then revenue; if respect, then respect; if honor, then honor (Rom. 13:1-7).

In Hebrews 13:17 these instructions are repeated: "Obey your leaders and submit to their authority." And the apostle Peter says, "Submit yourselves for the Lord's sake to every authority" (1 Pet. 2:13).

So What's the Problem?

Why have these statements caused such great difficulty? First, and most troubling, they seem to contradict other parts of the Bible. Second, we can all immediately think of certain evil governments that surely ought *not* to be obeyed. Peter, when commanded by a pagan government to stop preaching the gospel replied, "We must obey God rather than men" (Acts 5:29). Shadrach, Meshach and Abednego, when ordered to bow down to the idols of King Nebuchadnezzar responded, "We will not serve your gods or worship the image of gold you have set up" (Dan. 3:18).

The prophet Daniel refused to obey King Darius's law prohibiting him from praying to the God of Israel (see Dan. 6:7-10). In all these instances of civil defiance, God showed His approval with miracles of deliverance.

It seems clear enough from these passages that God expects us to do just as Peter said, to "obey God rather than men" (Acts 5:29). We know very well that we are not to bow down to any other god; the second commandment says so. Similarly, we cannot obey a law that forbids our prayers. And since Jesus commands us to preach the gospel in every land, His instructions will certainly take precedence over any earthly law that says otherwise.

So far it sounds fairly simple; our formula for balancing Romans 13 with the rest of the Bible will be this: We will obey the laws of the land, but only if those man-made laws do not contradict God's laws. End of discussion? No. Unfortunately, it's often easier to state the formula than it is to follow it.

To see why let's apply our formula to the Ten Commandments (God's laws) and the Constitution of the United States (human laws). Commandment number one, "You shall have no other gods before me" (Exod. 20:3).

For many this creates a dilemma. In America some people have an attitude that approaches worship of the Constitution. That is, they invest it with an authority that extends over every other authority. The Constitution is seen as the very last word on all matters of national policy, even when those matters involve questions of morality.

This document is more a part of everyday life for many judges and lawyers than the Bible is for many Christians. Every law in every law book in the United States is ultimately subject to this one question: "Is it constitutional?" (not, "Is it biblical?"). Anyone who holds public office in the U.S. must be willing to swear (ironically, with one hand on the Bible) to support the Constitution. By this arrangement, the officeholder may be promising *to put God second in line* to the government. But because governments are man-made, they may contradict the Bible.

For example, at the time of this writing, the courts of the United States declare it lawful to kill unborn babies. (China has a similar law, but has gone one step further; there, unborn babies are killed whenever the *government* deems it necessary. And the citizens are expected to cooperate.)

The Conflict Widens

The problem of Constitution versus Bible involves more than just a few laws that happen to go against the laws of God. If it were a matter of one or two laws, we would simply ignore the few and obey the rest. But to give any earthly document the authority belonging only to the Word of God goes totally against the spirit of the first commandment. Christians cannot give their *unconditional* support to any human system of laws.

The Constitution of the United States is possibly the best document of its kind ever devised. But even given this fact, Christians must never put anything before God.

So what should Americans do? Renounce their citizenship? Certainly not. For one thing, they'd likely find themselves under a system vastly more hostile to Christianity than the one they live with. China and her mandatory abortion laws are only one example.

The Constitution of the United States is possibly the best document of its kind ever devised. But even given this fact, Christians must never put anything before God.

We can handle the second commandment with less difficulty: "You shall not make for yourself an idol" (Exod. 20:4). Most of us have few problems avoiding graven images, though many will suggest that we actually worship the images of our material possessions, like our Volvos, luxury appliances or multi-story town houses.

But when we get to the third commandment, "You shall not misuse the name of the Lord your God" (Exod. 20:7), we are in trouble again. For some, it is misuse of God's name to say, "one nation under God," while some are in bold defiance of God's laws. And others ask, Is it vain to print the words "In God We Trust" on our money, when "In Financial Security We Trust" would be closer to the truth?

Dual Allegiance Is Unworkable

No method of arranging a dual allegiance is workable. Christians cannot have 100 percent allegiance to God and also have 100 percent allegiance to a nation. Jesus said, "No one can serve two masters" (Matt. 6:24). And we can see He is right. This leads us to explore how we can both "submit . . . to the governing authorities" (Rom. 13:1) and "obey God rather than men" (Acts 5:29).

Romans 13 in the Ancient World

One way to gain insight on what it means to submit to the governing authorities is to look at what was going on when Paul wrote the letter to the Romans.

The original people who received this letter were the first century people of the church of Rome. Some modern writers believe that this church was made up primarily of Gentiles. Jews, however, constituted a portion of the congregation.

One of the purposes of Paul's letter was to explain the relationship of Jew to Gentile. Paul also shared with the Romans his deep concern for the nation of Israel and for the poverty-stricken Christians of Jerusalem (see 15:25-28). At the time, the church at Jerusalem was the hub of Christendom. Christians in other lands looked to it for leadership. In the area of the relationship between the Church and the state, however, the Jews had a tumultuous history.

The Jews were considered notoriously rebellious by other nations. Some Jewish sects, notably the Zealots, refused any cooperation with the pagan Romans who governed them. They refused to pay taxes and resorted to violence in attempting to overthrow Roman rule. The Zealots were strict traditionalists and nationalists who felt they owed allegiance to God alone. Early Christians might have been tempted to follow their example. But the conduct of the Zealots was in conflict with Christian principles (see Matt. 22:21; 1 Tim. 2:1-3; Titus 3:1; 1 Pet. 2:13,14). Paul used his letter to the Romans to strongly stress the correct relationship between Christians and the state.

Romans 13 Is for Today
But it just won't do to brush off the instructions in Romans 13 as though they were intended only for the Jews of the first century. The Bible is God's Word for all time. Therefore, God, through Paul, was making a point about Christian citizenship that applies not only to the Roman Christians, but to all Christians in all times. Paul was relating to Christians the instruction that God wants them to be model citizens. He expects the Church to be the cornerstone of civic order and stability.

Our Hope Is in Christ
The Christians's hope is set on Christ and His Kingdom, not on any worldly government or order. To set our hope on Christ is to put aside every other consideration (especially our egos) and follow His example of sacrificial service.

THE ANSWER: DO AS JESUS DOES

Whoever understands the meaning of sacrificial service has the answer to the mystery we are trying to unravel: The answer is found in total, undivided devotion to Christ, in radical, uncompromising discipleship.

According to John 19 Jesus found Himself a prisoner in the hands of Roman governor, Pilate. Pilate asked, "Don't you realize I have power either to free you or to crucify you?" (John 19:10). Jesus answered, "You would have no power over me if it were not given to you from above" (John 19:11).

Here we see that Jesus agreed with an important part of Paul's words on civic duty, "The authorities that exist have been established by God" (Rom. 13:1). Some have read Christ's words and concluded that He was condoning rebellion when He said this to Pilate. But just the opposite is true. Just a few hours earlier Jesus had said, "Do you think I cannot call on my Father, and he will at once put at my disposal more than twelve legions of angels?" (Matt. 26:53). But Jesus refused to revolt against the Roman government (much to the chagrin of the politically-minded reactionaries of His day).

There were also times when Jesus did not follow the dictates of Jewish law. He allowed His disciples to pick grain on the Sabbath (see Matt. 12:1). When the Pharisees criticized Him for allowing work on the day of rest, Jesus rebuked them saying, "If you had known what these words mean, 'I desire mercy, not sacrifice,' you would not have condemned the innocent. For the Son of Man is Lord of the Sabbath" (Matt. 12:7,8). In this statement Jesus asserted His authority to overrule the Pharisees' unmerciful interpretations of the fourth commandment (see Exod. 20:8-10).

On another Sabbath Jesus healed a man whose hand was shriveled (see Luke 6:6-11). These examples help us understand one motivation God might consider proper for civil disobedience: mercy.

Sometimes sincere compassion may compel us to disobey the government. This was certainly the case with Corrie ten Boom and her family who hid Jews from the Nazis during World War II.

They disobeyed with meekness—something that is foreign to many of us.

Even though Jesus' example of meekness is familiar, it is easy to develop an attitude of pride about righteous behavior, especially if that behavior involves sacrifice or danger. If we disobey the government because we desire to appear strong or brave, our motivation is all wrong.

Our Pride Is Deadly

Pride is the deforming and enfeebling influence that makes the world go 'round in such a sick, lopsided fashion. Pride brought about Lucifer's fall from heaven. "Better to reign in hell," he says, in Milton's *Paradise Lost*, "than serve in Heav'n." Out of pride the first man and woman rejected paradise and chose disobedience. And the same hell-inspired notion misguides men and women in the twentieth century. It destroys marriages and starts world wars. And its influence is formidable as we respond to Romans 13. For many will disobey the government claiming to obey their consciences when, in fact, they are only obeying their pride.

Some, of course, make no pretense about conscience. They defy the government merely for convenience sake. Some break the law in order to save themselves money. They cheat on their income taxes (or refuse to pay them altogether) and feel no shame whatever in doing so. But we have our hands full addressing those who at least *suppose* themselves to be following their consciences. To those who make no such claims, we have nothing to say. They would profit little by it if we did.

When Should We Disobey?

We still haven't answered the question of exactly where Christians ought to draw the line between duty to God and duty to the government. How should Christians respond to a government that is entirely corrupt, a government that commands its citizens to act in ways that blatantly contravene the laws of God?

Jesus' Answer

Jesus answers these questions by appealing to the conscience—
something He spent a good deal of time talking about. In Matthew 9:13 He quoted the Old Testament: "I desire mercy, not sacrifice." *Sacrifice* refers to the many requirements of Jewish law.
But mercy, too, is one of the standards of God's laws. It also
must be obeyed, and those who have genuine mercy like the ten
Booms, need no one to tell them when to use it.

In Luke 12:57 Jesus posed a challenging question: "Why
don't you judge for yourselves what is right?" Here Jesus was
referring to the settling of civil disputes out of court. But He is
addressing a mind-set common to all of us. And it comes up
whenever we grapple with any apparent contradiction, such as
the one we find between Romans 13 and Acts 5:29.

Modern Pharisees

The problem with Romans 13 and its counterparts is simply
that many of us, like the Pharisees, are looking for rigid, black
and white rules. Rules leave the conscience undisturbed. Awak-
ening the conscience is dangerous business; it makes high and
strenuous demands on us that we are slow to meet. It takes us
far beyond the limits of written laws, and it may get us into hot
water with both religious and secular authorities. And why not?
For this is precisely what happened to Jesus.

It's no wonder we'd rather observe a rigid and predictable system of rules. That's the easy way to go. It requires only the lowest, pharisaical ways of thinking. But a healthy conscience,
inspired by the Holy Spirit, requires a heart like Christ's.

A New Question of Motive

The Pharisees in Jesus' time were caught up in the minute letter
of Jewish law. This law was carried out not for the love of God

but for the love of religion and for the purpose of avoiding personal blame. This brings us to an entirely new problem.

The problem is this: Many of us are slow to understand that the Bible was given as a means of knowing our heavenly Father and all the things that please Him. Instead, and sadly, we may think of it as a means of escaping from Him. Rather than drawing close to God, the modern Pharisee seeks protection *from* God in a set of legal contrivances.

We must ask ourselves the following questions: What is my motivation for obeying Romans 13? Is it because I want to please God? Or, do I simply want protection from His wrath?

A Motivation of Fear or Love?

Jesus compared the motivation of fear to the motivation of love in His parable about stewardship in Matthew 25. A servant was given one talent, which he was expected to put to good use on behalf of his master. But instead, he buried it for safekeeping, out of fear. "I knew that you are a hard man," he explained later, "I was afraid and went out and hid your talent in the ground" (Matt. 25:24,25).

Christ's compassion is the best answer we have to our dilemma of church versus state.

This servant was more concerned with staying out of trouble than with doing his duty. He was expected to make something of what he had been given, to invest it and show a profit. But he squandered an important opportunity because all he knew how to do was play it safe. And because he was afraid of losing what little he had, he lost even that. The one talent was taken away from him and he was left with nothing.

What paltry service we give to God if we act like that servant!

How sad it must make Him when we obey Him merely to secure our own safety! God does not want self-serving, hollow gestures of obedience. He wants us to know who He is, to love Him for it and to obey Him because our hearts will settle for nothing less. He wants us to be like Christ, who is willing to suffer and die and take false blame for compassion's sake.

Christ's compassion is the best answer we have to our dilemma of church versus state. If we would be His disciples, Jesus would have us obey Romans 13 by all possible means, within the context of total, sacrificial obedience—obedience of the sort Jesus Himself practiced daily.

There is no formula that will enable us to draw a firm, black line between God's laws and human laws. There is no system that will show us when we are bound to obey the government and when we are bound to obey only God. But God has given His Holy Spirit, along with an instrument to hear Him with, the conscience. He expects us to listen to Him, and He holds us accountable. God wants us to let the Holy Spirit guide us into genuine devotion to Him, doing everything in our power to imitate Christ. Under no other circumstances may we say with Peter, "We must obey God rather than men."

11

Terrorism— What Is Our Response?

TRACY L. SCOTT

Terrorism. A frightening word. A frustrating word. A word that leaves us helpless in our anger. What is there about terrorism that could possibly hold "the other half of the story"?

At first glance, terrorism seems to be a black and white moral issue. It simply is wrong. But the closer we look at the realities of terrorism, the harder it is to pronounce facile judgment on this problem. For instance:

> One of the Shiite gunmen who hijacked the TWA flight 847 in June 1985 went up and down the aisle of the plane saying, "New Jersey, New Jersey." One of the terrified passengers, apparently hoping to establish common ground, said, "Hey, I'm from Jersey." Not much came of that; the gunman went to the back of the plane, and before long he

shot a U.S. navy diver. He was about to shoot a second one when, upon the intervention of a stewardess, the diver said, "I have a wife and daughter." The Shiite gunman said, "Yes, so did I. They were killed in the shelling of our village in Lebanon by the U.S.S. New Jersey."[1]

The gunman, here, sought revenge for a seemingly evil act of murder against his wife and child. He took the law into his own hands to exercise a sort of vigilante justice. He terrorized innocent people and killed a U.S. navy diver. He is certainly a terrorist. But can we say that his actions were not justifiable in any way? This is a difficult question. And this situation illustrates the complexities of the whole issue of terrorism.

In order to deal objectively with the issue, we must avoid stereotypes. People tend to stereotype terrorists in one of two ways. Some see all terrorists as evil thugs given to mindless violence. They are viewed as being either crazy or controlled by fanatical leaders. Other people see terrorists as misguided idealists who have become so frustrated with the oppressive situation under which they live that they resort to violence. There is some truth in both of these views.[2] But what we must remember is that terrorists are not all alike. Motivations, methods and goals differ among various terrorist groups and individuals. And our emotional support of or opposition to a group's purposes will color our image of them. For as it has been said: One person's "terrorist" is another person's "freedom fighter."

This brings us to the crucial problem of definitions. If we as Christians and as the Church want to determine our position on terrorism, then we must first define terrorism.

TOWARDS A DEFINITION OF TERRORISM

The most characteristic feature of terrorism is its random violence against innocent people. Victims are not targeted because of specific things that they have done, but rather because of who they are. Thus, whole populations or nations fall prey to the terrorists' anger and violence. If the terrorist group believes that a certain government is oppressing them, then anyone who is a citizen of that country or supports its government is seen as an enemy and target.[3] For example, when Iranian students took Americans hostage at the U.S. Embassy in Tehran in 1979, they were reacting to the United States' support of the Shah whom they regarded as oppressive. The students considered these Americans fair game by the mere fact that they were U.S. citizens.

This example brings up another feature of terrorism. Terrorist acts are not done for the mere sake of violence, but in order to accomplish some political end. The terrorists use violence to try to bring about solutions to perceived injustices against them. Because superpower nations have a tendency to dominate world affairs, some small nations feel that their only recourse to being heard is through terrorism. James Sterba offers a good general definition of terrorism: "Terrorism is the use or threat of violence against innocent people to further some political objective."[4]

Most government officials, scholars and citizens would agree on this definition of terrorism, but not all people agree on to whom it is applied. Many people would like to find a way to apply this definition only to groups who are enemies of their own government. They would like to avoid examining their actions or the acts of friends and allies in light of this definition of terrorism. Take, for example, the situation in Nicaragua. It is easy for some to label certain acts of the Sandinistas as terrorist. But when innocent people are killed as a result of the Contras' struggle, it is perceived by these same people as an unavoidable and regrettable mistake. On the other side of the political spectrum the Sandinistas may be excused for their violence and seen as the liberators of the Nicaraguan people. To people of this political persuasion, it is the Contras who are held responsible for violent acts against the populace. Who is right?

Regardless of the right or wrong motivations of these two opposing groups, their actions must be judged by the same criteria. If we agree on the basic definition of terrorism, then both of these groups are engaging in terrorist acts if they kill innocent people to achieve their goals. If we agree that killing innocent people (which at the very least means children) is wrong, then we must denounce all acts which aim violence at the innocent members of a society. However, if we believe that the end still may sometimes justify evil means, then we would have to examine **all** terrorist acts to see if the consequences are righteous enough to justify evil means.

A VARIETY OF RESPONSES

We've defined what terrorism is. But what should governments (and other groups in the war against terrorism) do about it?

The complexities of terrorism make responses to it difficult to determine. No one seems to agree on what the best response is. There have been various responses to the terrorism of the Irish Republican Army (IRA) fighting for the independence of Northern Ireland from Great Britain. The British government has repeatedly used force against IRA members. At the same time, it has tried to negotiate with the legal, political arm of the IRA.

This example shows how responses to terrorism generally fall into one of two categories: military or political. Military responses aim at eliminating terrorists by means of force. Here, the terrorists are seen as criminals who should be punished. Their political objectives are either discounted or regarded as wrong.

Political responses recognize the grievances of terrorists and try to stop the terrorists by negotiating over their demands. Those who advocate political responses believe that if the causes of terrorist dissatisfaction are dealt with, then terrorist acts will stop.[5]

The role of the Church is to offer guidance in evaluating morality. This should include the morality of responses to terrorism, as well as evaluating terrorism itself.

The debate over the best response to terrorism usually focuses on what will be most effective in ending terrorism, although many people believe that containing terrorist acts is the best we will ever do. Still, responses are usually measured by effectiveness and not morality. Christians must, instead, evaluate responses to terrorism in both moral and practical terms. An analysis of the effectiveness of different responses is best left to public policy specialists. However, the role of the Church is to offer guidance in evaluating morality. This should include the morality of responses to terrorism, as well as evaluating terrorism itself.

HOW DOES THE CHURCH EVALUATE TERRORISM?

It is understood that violence is the crucial problem in the whole issue of terrorism. Over the centuries, the Church has struggled to come to terms with the morality of violence in the context of war. In order to answer the question, How does the Church evaluate terrorism? We can gain insight by considering the three major positions that Christians take regarding war:

The Crusade position believes that God uses war as an instrument of justice. This view is based on the Old Testament and God's use of Israel to punish evil people and nations. (A fact less often cited is that God also used other countries to discipline Israel.) Likewise, God can use contemporary nations to do His will. Military solutions should be used to promote good and defeat evil.

At the opposite extreme are Christian pacifists. The Pacifist position is based on the New Testament emphasis on love, especially on Jesus' Sermon on the Mount in which Jesus calls us to practice love instead of violence when confronted by enemies (see Matt. 5:39-48). Pacifists believe that violence is never a right strategy for those who belong to the Kingdom of God.[6]

In between these two extremes is the Just War position. (The criteria for this position were developed by Augustine A.D. 354-430.) Here, military force is not seen as an ordinary means of promoting justice, but rather as a last resort to combat evil when all else fails. War and violence, themselves, are never right, as the commandment forbids us to murder (see Exod. 20:13), and Jesus tells us to turn the other cheek (see Matt. 5:39).

However, in Romans 13 Paul tells us that the state can be God's agent to punish evil (see v. 4). To people who hold the Just War position, war is to be used if it is the lesser of two evils. This position believes that war can be just if it meets certain criteria: The cause must be just; the use of violence must be a last resort; there must be a high probability of success and; the means of force used must be limited and controlled.[7]

This last criterion points out a crucial difference between the Just War and the Crusade positions. Both of these positions would say that the goals of military action must be just. But the Just War position calls us to bring moral considerations to bear on the actual use of violence. The enemy is not combatted "at any cost." Rather, there are limitations to military force: The violence used must be less than that which it is supposed to remedy, and violence is directed only at combatants and military targets—never at civilians.[8] One must keep in mind that in contemporary times many weapons make no distinction between combatants and the innocent. Thus, persons who hold to the

Just War Theory may be inclined to react as pacifists since the principles are difficult to apply.

So what do these three positions on war have to do with terrorism? As the Church seeks to address the problem of terrorism, its evaluations will most probably fall in line with its position on war. Thus, the Crusade position will look primarily at goals of both the terrorists and their opponents. If a cause is deemed to be good and just, then that group will be supported. If the cause is not just, then that group will be opposed by any means. And if a group attacks those nations representing just and righteous causes, then it must be opposed as evil. This position sees the world as a cosmic battleground for the forces of good (God) and evil (Satan).

For example, many Christians believe that the Nicaraguan Contras are fighting for a just cause: freedom, and against an evil force: the Communist Sandinistas. Thus the Contras are supported as "freedom fighters," although some question their methods, which they feel result in the killing of innocent civilians, and consider them terrorists. The question of violence (the means and methods) in this struggle is secondary to the question of whose cause is right.

Conversely, pacifists tend to focus on means rather than the ends. As Christians, they believe we are called not just to uphold the good, but to act always in a manner worthy of our Lord. Violence is never consistent with the loving and peacemaking actions to which Jesus has called us. Therefore, pacifists' evaluations of terrorism and responses to it will focus on the actions involved more than the objectives. The violence of terrorism will be denounced, as will any military action against it. No cause ever justifies the murder of human beings.

Just War proponents try to balance a concern for both means and ends. Christians of this position are very wary of violent actions, for they believe Scripture clearly advocates peace over war (see Matt. 5:9; Rom. 12:18; 1 Tim. 2:1,2). Yet they realize that there may be some evil that cannot go unchecked and that can be stopped only by military action. As Christians we should promote just and righteous ends, but only if the means to these ends have been subjected to moral and biblical considerations. Thus, this position will seek to evaluate both the means and ends of terrorist groups and the responses to them.

Often, terrorist groups have just causes and legitimate grievances. For example, the PLO's desire for its own homeland is viewed by many as being legitimate. Its objective of self-governance is an ideal which the United States has frequently championed. Then, are the PLO's violent actions justifiable because the goals are legitimate? According to Just War theory, no, because the PLO's violence does not meet moral or biblical criteria. The PLO has used violence indiscriminately (that is, against innocent civilians), and thus, their actions cannot be justified. Righteous goals do not justify the evil of these means.

Then what about the responses to terrorism? Can military action ever be justified in order to stop terrorism? Again, both goals and means must be evaluated. First, the goals must be just and righteous. Are we seeking to punish and stop the terrorists' killing of innocent people? Romans 13 says that the state is justified in punishing evildoers. And certainly if military action will end the future violence of terrorists, then it could be justifiable. But how does a nation take action against terrorists?

The means of the responses to terrorism must also be just. Some people advocate using military violence against the supposed bases of terrorist activity. This seems to be the reasoning behind President Reagan's order to bomb Colonel Kadafi's headquarters in the Libyan city of Tripoli. Libya was perceived as a training ground for terrorists, and Colonel Kadafi a supporter of those groups. So, in the wake of increased violence against Americans, President Reagan took aim at this base of terrorist activity. However, Jim Miller, staff writer for *Newsweek*, writes that there was no proof that any actual terrorists were in Libya at the time, nor was there any certainty that the attack would truly get rid of proven evildoers. (However, since the time of the bombing, Kadafi's terrorists' activities have been deterred.) Rather, the risks of killing innocent civilians were substantial, and in fact 30 civilians were killed.[9] Thus, according to Just War theory and Miller's report, the raid on Libya cannot be justified, since the means failed to adequately discriminate between the innocent and the guilty. To those who support this theory, violent retaliation must only be used as a last resort and only if there is no risk to innocent civilians.

We must understand that the Christian use of Just War theory is an attempt to fulfill the biblical command to love our neighbors (see Lev. 19:18; Matt. 19:19). Sometimes, the command to love means that we must use force to stop an enemy from injuring the innocent. However, any military force used must be aimed at the evildoer. With terrorism, we must be sure that we do not harm the "enemy's" innocent people in order to protect "ours."

THE CHURCH'S POSITION

As we have seen, terrorism is a complex issue, and the Church's position on this issue is not clear nor settled. As long as Christians continue to differ over the right use of violence, the Church will not have a unified position on terrorism. However, there are some fundamental points which we, as Christians, can agree upon.

First, the horror which God shows towards the shedding of innocent blood (see Prov. 6:16,17) should be a horror which we all share. And this should translate into the actions we support.

Second, as Christians we must all seek to love our neighbors as well as to promote justice and peace. Practically, this means that we need to hold love and justice together as we relate not only to our friends but also to our enemies. Loving our neighbors means that we not only try to protect the innocent, but also that we listen to our enemies to see if there is any truth in their position. Specifically, we need to take terrorists' grievances seriously. Some of their causes and grievances address real injustice. We must deal with the *legitimate* complaints of the terrorists if true justice and peace are to prevail.

Third, whatever biblical and moral principles we use to assess terrorism, we must also apply to our own country's response to terrorism. If we denounce the methods used by terrorists, then in good conscience we cannot use the same methods to combat terrorism. We must examine our own goals and methods as carefully as we examine our enemies'. As Christ's representatives on earth, we cannot be hypocritical in our moral stance.

As a prophetic witness, the Church should continually bring biblical principles to bear on the public debate about terrorism.

Finally, whatever a specific church's position is on terrorism, all believers should encourage biblical thinking on this issue. As a prophetic witness, the Church should continually bring biblical principles to bear on the public debate about terrorism. We need to get beyond slogans and stereotypes and call for public honesty in the discussion of terrorism. Rather than simply endorsing or denouncing various politicians and public policies, the Church should encourage Christians to look at this issue critically.

However, "when the church concludes that biblical faith or righteousness requires it to take a public stand on some issue, then it must obey God's Word and trust him with the consequences."[10] Whether a "public stand" means teaching and proclaiming or corporate political action will depend on the various Christian groups' traditions. But whatever our churches decide to do, as individuals responsible to God, we must always seek to be informed about the world and to respond to its complexities, biblically and prayerfully. We must never cease to be involved in and to pray for the world which God has created and loves. For the "world is the arena in which we are to live and love, witness and serve, suffer and die for Christ."[11]

Notes

1. Moorhead Kennedy, "The Root Causes of Terrorism," *Morality in Practice*, 2nd ed., ed. James P. Sterba, (Belmont, CA: Wadsworth Publishing Co., 1988), p. 402.

2. Conor Cruise O'Brien, "Thinking About Terrorism," *Morality in Practice*, pp. 410,411.

3. Michael Walzer, *Just and Unjust Wars* (New York: Basic Books,1977), pp. 197-200.

4. James P. Sterba, Introduction to "Terrorism" section, *Morality in Practice*, p. 392.

5. Ibid., pp. 393-395.

6. Mark R. Amstutz, *Christian Ethics and U.S. Foreign Policy* (Grand Rapids: Academic Books, Zondervan, 1987), pp. 92,93.

7. John Stott, *Issues Facing Christians Today* (Basingstoke, Eng.: Marshalls, 1984), pp. 84-88.

8. Ibid., p. 85.

9. Jim Miller, "The War That Reagan Lost," *Newsweek*, August 29, 1988, pp. 60,62.

10. "Evangelism and Social Responsibility: An Evangelical Commitment," *The Grand Rapids Report* (Grand Rapids: Paternoster, 1982), p. 52, quoted in Stott, *Issues*, p. 13.

11. Stott, *Issues*, p. 26.

Practical Action _____

As individual Christians and local churches, what can we do about the question of terrorism?

1. **Develop political awareness about the issue at stake, both personally and as a church.** Before we can study terrorism biblically, we must first understand the realities involved.

- Christians who are especially concerned about this issue could form or join a group to study terrorism in more depth. This group could be part of the local church, inviting "experts" in to discuss various aspects of terrorism.
- Christians could join a "secular" political group to keep informed and lend biblical input.
- Christians could take a class that deals with the issues of terrorism and military violence.

2. **Evaluate the issues of terrorism in light of biblical principles.** Christians must not stop with an intellectual understanding of terrorism, but must seek to bring biblical principles to bear on this issue.

- It is often difficult for individual Christians to form biblical responses to all of the many issues which confront us in the world, so formation of a "special interest" or "study and action" group would be very helpful. This group would develop a biblical perspective on the issue of terrorism, specifically, or maybe the larger issues of war and peace. Then the group could report back to the larger church.
- The church could encourage discussion of terrorism, with the group members acting as "experts."
- Group members and/or church members would take any action that the church agrees is necessary.

3. **Pray.**
- Pray for leaders in charge of responding to terrorists.

ists.

- Pray for specific situations of terrorist activity.
- Pray for protection of the innocent.

Assassination: Should We Stay the Good Guys?* _____

Assassination has an emotional appeal when people are frightened, frustrated and angry. Terrorist attacks have worn down our patience with so-called experts who constantly remind us that combatting terrorism is a difficult and enduring task. But there is right and wrong, and there is good and evil, and we are supposed to be the good guys. If assassination can be justified, why must it always be covert? Why must our roles be concealed? And why does the word get stuck in our throats? On the other hand, can we minimize the loss of life—the lives of future victims of terrorism as well as the lives of innocent bystanders who might be killed in a conventional military response—by killing those who most directly influence their behavior? Why not assassination?

Here are arguments in favor of assassination as a means of combatting terrorism, followed by arguments against it.

1. **Assassination may preclude greater evil.** "Wouldn't you have assassinated Adolf Hitler?" proponents often ask. With hindsight, it's easy to say, "Yes, of course." But how do we identify future Hitlers? Regrettably, his attributes are not so unusual among world leaders.

2. **Assassination produces fewer casualties than retaliation with conventional weapons.**

3. **Assassination of terrorist leaders would disrupt terrorist groups more than any other form of attack.**

4. **Assassination leaves no prisoners to become causes for further terrorist attacks.**

Against assassination are moral and legal constraints, operational difficulties and practical considerations:

1. **Assassination is morally wrong.** Can you imagine the President of the United States appearing on television to announce, "Some time ago I authorized the assassination of Moamar Kadafi. I am pleased to report that American agents have successfully carried out this mission."

2. **Assassination is illegal.** In the mid-1970s, President Ford issued an Executive Order: "No person employed or acting on behalf of the United States government shall engage in, or conspire to engage in, assassination." The president could lift this ban, but assassinating terrorist leaders means going into another sovereign country and killing someone. If British agents began gunning down IRA fund-raisers on the streets of Boston, we'd charge them with murder.

3. **In combatting terrorism we ought not to employ actions indistinguishable from those of the terrorists themselves.**

4. **Assassination of terrorists could justify further actions against us.**

5. **Our opponents have the advantage.** Terrorist leaders are elusive. In contrast, our leaders are particularly vulnerable.

6. **The replacement for the person we kill may be even worse.**

7. **Assassins may have their own agendas.** Assassination is a nasty business, and it often requires employing nasty people. We would have to rely on third parties whose political agendas and attitudes about violence might differ from our own.

8. **In the long run, it doesn't work.** Following the bloody attack on Israeli athletes at the Munich Olympics in 1972, Israel embarked upon a campaign of assassination, killing 11 known or suspected leaders of Palestinian terrorist organizations. The campaign ended after an innocent waiter in Norway was killed, mistakenly identified as a terrorist on the list. It was difficult to

discern any decline in Palestine terrorist attacks at the time, and Israelis and Jews worldwide are still targets.

Sometimes military force may be a necessary response to terrorism. The death of a terrorist leader during a commando assault on a terrorist training camp would cause no qualms. But there is still a crucial difference between a covert military operation and assassination—the cold-blooded murder of a specific individual.

By Brian Jenkins
Public Domain

*This material is presented to help the reader apply the biblical reasoning given in the chapter to a critical current issue. For this reason, we've not attempted to inject biblical argument, but leave that to the reader.

12

Putting the Brakes on Sexual Sin

CHARLES MYLANDER[1]

Ever since God created male and female, each sex has found something fascinating about the other. At its best, this powerful attraction leads to some of life's profound joys: romances catch fire, marriages mature and healthy friendships between men and women flourish. At its worst, misused sex leads to ugly wounds and lasting scars: romances decay into bitter routines, marriages end in divorce and once-healthy friendships decline into conflict or immorality. Sooner or later almost every Christian struggles with sexual temptation. Very few escape this battle without a skirmish or two. Some fight the war every day.

Sex as God planned it leads to much of the best in life. Bonding of personalities, delightful children and satisfying pleasure all come from pure sex within marriage and controlled sexuality outside of marriage. Immoral sex, on the other hand, ignites emotional explosions, burns personalities, leaves ugly scars and sometime ends in death.

THE STRESS OF SEXUAL TEMPTATION

It is by no means the only enticement to sin, but sexual temptation plagues many. *Time* magazine reports that for millions it
causes great stress.

> When psychiatrist George Serban of New York University
> conducted a nationwide poll of 1,008 mostly married men
> and women aged 18-60, he found that the greatest source
> of stress was the changes in society's attitudes toward sex,
> including sexual permissiveness and "the new social role of
> the sexes."[2]

Stress comes not only from seeing these changes in others but
also from personal wars with sexual temptation, especially when
guilt follows a moral defeat. I know, firsthand. I am not especially
proud of my own inner war. For years I struggled with lustful
thoughts. They plagued my mind and irritated my soul. Nothing
seemed to help for long; not self-discipline, not prayer, not Bible
memorization, not new experiences with God, not anything. I
felt I had no one to talk to about my private battle with lust. In
fact, I began to think that no answers existed.

THE BATTLEGROUND

This was the battleground, not the rose garden, of my Christian
growth. I prayed during these times of struggle and defeat; God
knows I prayed. The Lord answered my prayer, too, at the
moment. I confessed my sins often and repented (or at least I
thought I did) more times than I can recall.

Nothing seemed to give lasting relief. Guilt and discourage-
ment dogged my steps. Yet there was no question in my mind
that I belonged to Jesus Christ. He had touched my life and, in
spite of my inner struggles, I experienced a daily fellowship with
Him.

NEW HOPE

The turning point for me came when I viewed a Christian film about a different subject altogether. In the film was one short prayer that grabbed my attention: "Lord Jesus, protect me by your blood." In a flash of insight, I knew that Christ's power was as near to me as that quick prayer.

Believe me, my thought life turned around. For six months I was rigid in my self-discipline. The simple prayer, "Lord Jesus, protect me by your blood," came often to my lips or thoughts. I prayed it with authority and meant it from my innermost heart.

God honored it and a strange thing happened. The temptation did not just vaporize, but its power was broken. When I prayed, something like an invisible curtain came down between me and the lustful thought. It was not a solid curtain, but one that blocked enough of the tempting sight that I was able to resist it if I so chose.

Obedience to God became a daily pattern and then lasting victory came year after year. I was not perfect. I encountered some brief setbacks and at times I slipped. But the trend of my life with Christ was trust and obedience. With every inner victory came renewed joy and restored confidence.

Spiritual warfare on some front—temptation, suffering or service—will face every Christian. The truth is that we won't come to maturity in the Christian life until we begin obeying God at our point of greatest struggle. This is our own battleground.

HOLY-GROUND EXPERIENCES

My story does not end here. No soldier spends all his time on the battleground. In His sovereignty, our beloved King also leads us, His children, on to "holy ground." In fact, the more time I spend on holy ground the more effective I become on the battleground.

The Bible reminds me that our gracious God wants to do far more in the life of each Christian than we can ask or imagine (see Eph. 3:20,21). My holy-ground times come when I meet God in a life-changing way.

As you read these words, you may recall holy-ground moments, quiet or stunning, when God moved in. How can you forget them? You are never quite the same again.

THE SPURTS AND LONG HAUL OF IT ALL

Most committed followers of Jesus Christ understand both holy-ground and battleground kinds of growth. Sometimes God makes Himself known in striking ways, convincing us of His power and presence—holy ground. At other times He allows trials and temptations that dog our steps to the point of despair—battleground. Holy-ground growth comes in dramatic spurts. Battleground growth follows the long hard pull. Holy-ground experiences sometimes lead to exhilarating times with God. Battleground progress comes from slugging it out with temptation day after day, learning the hard way how Christ turns a loser into a winner.

Not one of us will come to maturity in the Christian life until we begin to win the struggle on our unique battleground.

For constant progress in the Christian life, winning on the battleground is more important than searching for a new holy ground. *Not one of us will come to maturity in the Christian life until we begin to win the struggle on our unique battleground.* Whatever the temptation—an unruly tongue, misused money, a shattered relationship, a bad attitude or misguided sexual attraction—only those who overcome will reach maturity in their lives with Christ. Whether our temptation is in the mind or the body, the way to win is to trust God on the holy ground and obey Him on the battleground.

CHRIST'S RESPONSE TO SEXUAL SIN

The Bible teaches that the Lord has a heart for our human weaknesses (see Ps. 103:13,14; Heb. 4:15,16). What these verses teach is that Christ offers love, grace and forgiveness. The Lord is compassionate and eager to give refuge when no one else understands. In His life on earth, Christ revealed both compassion and conviction when it came to sexual sins (see John 8:1-11).

With God, your past is never so full of mistakes, failures and sins that your future is hopeless. Christ loves you, no matter what you have done. In fact, He delights in forgiving the worst of sex sins and rebuilding the lives of those who suffer its consequences. The Bible gives us plenty of examples:

- With David, it was adultery
- With Samson, it was compulsive lust
- With Gomer, Hosea's wife, it was a series of illicit affairs
- With some Corinthians, it was homosexual sin
- With an unnamed church member in Corinth, it was incest.

MORE THAN WILLPOWER

Once we trust Christ on the holy ground, we become ready to obey Him on the battleground. It will never be a piece of cake; Christ promised an abundant life, not an easy one. It will also take willpower, but willpower alone will never win the battle. Only Christ can open the door to the cage of sexual bondage. You may find it difficult to relate in any deep way with *my* struggles, for sexual temptation does not bother you as much as some other battle. But whatever the battle may be, what gives us *all* hope is this: Jesus meets us at our point of greatest need. This holds true even if our lack of willpower involves adultery and running the red lights.

RUNNING THE RED LIGHTS

Anyone looking for an affair can always find one. In the climate of today's society, adultery is easy to come by. What comes as a surprise to many is that Christians may fall into extramarital affairs even when they are not looking for them. Too often well-meaning believers make unwise moves and suddenly realize they are in love with someone other than their spouses. The "If I had only known what was happening . . . " revelation dawns too late.

NEGLECTFUL BEGINNINGS

A married Christian can cause pure sex to catch fire and build a wall of protection around his/her spouse. This involves building attention and love into the marriage every day. Compliments, tender talk, resolving conflict, meeting needs, coping with stress, forgiving and starting over are all a part of a good marriage. The most common cause of an affair is neglect. For example, a husband may provide well for his family's financial needs yet neglect his wife's heartfelt need to be cherished. Any major area of continued neglect gives the devil a foothold to tempt the other spouse toward infidelity.

A DANGEROUS DETOUR

Unwary Christians often become vulnerable because the tender talk with their own spouses is missing. Surface subjects like "Pass the toast" and "The weather is nice today, isn't it?" become all too typical. It may start with a sexual problem they no longer talk about. Then the finances pose trouble and the only communication is a fight. If a discipline problem with one of the kids continues and each blames the other, they touch the limit. Soon almost no tender talk takes place between them. Neither is there genuine sharing of real feelings about each other, about their goals or their hurts in life.

Then, with another employee or a neighbor, one of them begins confiding in someone of the opposite sex. This person, often divorced or hurting in his or her own marriage, listens intently and seems to care. Nothing in the conversation seems to hint of any immoral activity. Each feels it is innocent, harmless and even helpful to the other. Tender talk about real feelings, and often about marriage problems, is going on outside of marriage and not within it. The married spouse begins to lose respect in the inner chambers of the thought life. Yet the outsider who listens and cares moves up the ladder of likability.

THE LIGHT TURNS AMBER

Before long "innocent" touching begins taking place. If she is his secretary, he puts a hand on her shoulder while giving instructions. If he is a friend, there's a social embrace, a warm pat, a friendly nudge. Both would insist nothing is wrong with the limited physical contact between them because it is not related to sex. In fact, sometimes they are not even aware of how much innocent touching is going on. Yet in the new friendship, each is aware of the other's genuine admiration and acceptance.

THE LIGHT TURNS RED

Mark the principle well. When emotional delight and "innocent" touching come from outside the marriage, the light is changing from amber to red. Every driver knows this signal means put on the brakes. We cannot change our feelings in an instant, but we can change our actions. We can decide whom we will see and under what conditions. We can decide whether or not to send a card or note. We can control whom we talk to on the telephone. By taking the right actions and making no provision for wrong desires, we can slow down and stop before the light turns red (see Rom. 13:14).

If neither the man nor the woman puts on the brakes, the wrong relationship enters the next stage. The couple begins spending time together. At first, they just happen to work on the same projects, or they end up at the same events. It feels good to be together. But before long, the two are making excuses to spend extra hours with each other. Lunch or dinner, special gifts and hidden times for just the two of them soon become the norm.

By now both know they have much more than a casual friendship. They rationalize that it is not adultery because, after all, they are not sleeping together. A solid red light is glowing. Once an emotional affair is underway, the danger becomes intense.

The man wakes up to his erotic and emotional feelings of "love" for this other woman, although he tells himself he also loves his wife. The woman knows she is "madly in love" with this other man and often feels she made a mistake about the man she did marry. By this time, the two who are bound emotionally become one in the flesh. No more warning lights—the "accident" has occurred (see Exod. 20:14).

POWER TO TURN AROUND

Watching for the lights can warn us about the impending danger of temptation. To overcome, a Christian must want God's best at any cost. The bottom line in winning over sexual temptations is death to sin, death to selfish desires and life in Christ (see Rom. 6; Eph. 2:1-10; Col. 2:13—3:24).

The apostle Paul presents three concepts to highlight this truth—fact, faith and force.

Fact

The fact is "that our old self was crucified with him so that the body of sin might be rendered powerless, that we should no longer be slaves to sin" (Rom. 6:6). Every genuine Christian is to know, not feel, this fact. A Christian has been crucified with Christ and Christ lives in him (see Gal. 2:20).

Faith

Faith grabs hold of redemptive history, makes a personal union with Christ's death and resurrection, and applies it to life now. "In the same way, count yourselves dead to sin but alive to God in Christ Jesus" (Rom. 6:11). By faith, figure out the effects of your own death to sin. See yourself as unresponsive to misguided sexual appeal or to emotional warmth from the wrong person. Then consider yourself alive to God in Christ Jesus, appropriating His resurrection power to win over temptation. This step of faith is the turning point between victory and defeat.

Force

With the facts of God's Word in mind and with faith claiming Christ's life and power, the Christian must put his resources into force. This is a call for obedience (see Rom. 6:12,13). With each action the Christian chooses to make the parts of his body a force for God or a force for Satan. The thoughts of one's brain, the gaze of one's eyes, the words of one's tongue, the touch of one's caress must all be yielded to God. What a Christian does with the physical parts of his or her body shows whether or not faith is put into force.

A Christian can never conquer the one sin that gets him down until he loves the Lord Jesus more than that sin. Then he will repudiate his sin and turn to Jesus, his greater love. Even then, the alert Christian will build practices into his life-style that keep him or her out of an extramarital or premarital trap. We should note that the guidelines apply to both heterosexual and homosexual temptations.

TAKING CHARGE OF YOUR DIRECTION

Thought Control
The best place to win over sexual temptation, or any lack of self-control, is in the mind. Paul's command to "be transformed by the renewing of your mind" is the key in Romans 12:2. He also directs us to let our minds dwell on "whatever is noble, whatever is right, whatever is pure" (see Phil. 4:8). I have often found that a good defense against lust is to turn my thoughts at once to Christ. Quoting Scripture, mental prayers and meditating on the best things in life all help. At this point, however, it is vital to note that adultery gets its first foothold in one's thoughts.

At what point in one's thoughts does sexual attraction become mental adultery? In the Sermon on the Mount, the Lord Jesus taught: "Anyone who looks at a woman lustfully has already committed adultery with her in his heart" (Matt. 5:28). The context shows He is exposing the *intent of the heart.* Whenever a man looks at a woman with the intent of sinning sexually, he is into lust. If he says, "If I could get away with it, I would." The intent of his heart is sinful. When a woman thinks, *For this guy I'd do almost anything, I'm in love with him and he's in love with me, I want him, no matter what it takes* (and means an affair), the intent of her heart is adultery. Sinful lust is mental adultery springing from the heart's desire. Even before the point of actual sin, we can follow the Holy Spirit's prompting to keep our thoughts in the right place.

In most cases, a person plays with the idea of love, romance and sex with someone other than his spouse long before he takes any action. Mental adultery always precedes physical adultery. Subtle lies such as "God wants me to be happy" and "God will forgive me" begin to excuse wrong actions. They erode the resistance to sin.

J. Allan Petersen summarizes what happens next: "So our minds feed the fantasy, the fantasy creates the emotions, and the emotions scream for the actual experience. This is why when one is emotionally committed to an affair, all the truth and logic in the world don't seem to faze him. In a contest between emotion and truth, emotion usually wins."[3]

What a Christian does with his thought life will determine what he says and does in other parts of his behavior. Through the apostle Paul the Holy Spirit commands, "Set your minds on things above, not on earthly things" (Col. 3:2). "Things above" relate to Christ and all that pleases Him. "Earthly things" refer to the attitudes and actions that the Christian is to put aside and consider dead. Included in the Bible's list of earthly things that a Christian must not spend his time thinking or doing anything about are "immorality, impurity, lust, evil desires" (Col. 3:5).

The Christian mind-set is our most important discipline. Prayer, Bible study, Christian fellowship and obedience to the Holy Spirit all help us to keep our minds in the right place.

Word Control

In winning bouts with sexual temptation, thought control is only the first line of defense. Word control comes next. A wise Christian husband will make a personal pact never to share love language or tender talk with someone other than his mate. This includes a note or card in the mail and even a phone call just to talk.

Word control may also involve whom you speak with when discussing a relationship. A good guideline is: "Never take counsel from losers." In matters of morals and sex, a person picks up the values of those he or she listens to. If a person listens to those who have been losing the moral battle for a long time, he will likely follow their example. But if he takes his counsel from winners, he will probably learn how to overcome.

Touch Control

Thought control and word control are next to impossible without touch control. Within families healthy touching has its benefits. Children who grow up with lots of hugs and kisses from parents build a greater resistance to promiscuity. The tingle from touching a boyfriend or girlfriend seems less demanding for those who have no inner need to be stroked.

However, without careful controls, touching can lead to disaster outside of the family circle. Touching the opposite sex in casual relationships is now so common that many people are blind to its dangers.

What are a Christian's guidelines about touch? It's a simple matter of not touching someone of the opposite sex *when it brings comfort or inner delight.* As my pastor, C. W. Perry, once said, "If you are looking forward to the next hug, you are in big trouble."

When it comes to touching, another key word is discretion (see Prov. 11:22). The discreet use of touching can radiate the love of Christ, but without discretion the dangers are greater than most people imagine.

GETTING OFF THE DETOUR

What if all this talk about avoiding an affair comes too late? What if the adulterous relationship is already in full swing? How does someone break it off and get out?

The truth is that affairs blow up faster than marriages. Much of the appeal of an affair is fun and games without the burden of responsibility. As the relationship progresses, the expectations of one or both of the participants begin to rise. The grass may look greener on the other side of the fence, but it still has to be mowed. Tensions begin to build within the affair. The wrong relationship is built on a shifty foundation of deceit and adultery. It is not unusual for an affair to collapse. This means a faithful spouse needs extraordinary patience. When the time is right, however, one of those in the affair will want to break it up. What counsel can help them?

Amputation

The best way to break off an affair is to amputate. Because sex makes two people "one flesh" (see 1 Cor. 6:16), an amputation will cause intense pain. It is impossible to break up an affair without someone getting hurt. God never wants more pain directed toward our marriages. He always wants the adultery amputated rather than the marriage bond severed. It all boils down to somehow saying, "We must part forever. I cannot go on with this relationship."

Grief

The next stage, grieving, seems to come as a shock to many who leave an affair, and two surprises follow. The first is that the marriage seems less satisfying than the affair. The problems that built up for years and were intensified by adultery do not vanish overnight. It will take months to rebuild the marriage until it fully satisfies. Both partners must remind themselves often that their marriage is worth all the time and effort invested until it pays rich dividends.

The second surprise is that strong feelings of attraction, affection and desire for the one involved in the affair persist for a long time. Because adultery means a person has become one flesh with two partners, he or she will often feel torn in two, trapped, caught in the middle, confused and not sure whom he/she loves most. Misplaced affections must be reset like a fractured bone. Instead of bouncing back and forth between spouse and lover, the wise step is to set the splintered bone with a cast of grief.

To grieve well is to face up to recurring emotional cycles of distress, pain and loneliness. In fact, it is a rare exception when a person does not go through this grieving process. Since this is a normal part of God's healing, it is always right to turn to Him for comfort and relief. The Lord never wants the grieving person to return to the adulterous affair.

Healing

The final stage, healing, will certainly come. For those who return to a marriage, an interesting surprise often waits. Maybe it is God's reward to the faithful spouse. The renewed marriage often develops into a deeply satisfying relationship, far better than before. Please do not misunderstand. The adultery did not make the marriage better. Never. The determination to save the marriage, the spiritual growth that came to both spouses through crisis and the all-out efforts to rebuild God's intended relationship are what made it better. People in good marriages can invest this kind of effort without the devastation of adultery. The dividends for them are even higher.

No wonder Solomon penned these words in Proverbs 5:15-19:

Drink water from your own cistern,
running water from your own well.
Should your springs overflow in the streets,
your streams of water in the public squares?
Let them be yours alone,
never to be shared with strangers.
May your fountain be blessed,
and may you rejoice in the wife of your youth.
A loving doe, a graceful deer—
may her breasts satisfy you always,
may you ever be captivated by her love.

Notes

1. Adapted from Charles Mylander, *Running the Red Lights* (Ventura, CA: Regal Books, 1986).
2. *Time* magazine, June 6, 1983, p. 48.
3. J. Allan Petersen, *The Myth of the Greener Grass* (Wheaton: Tyndale House Publishers, Inc., 1983).

When the Brakes Fail: Results of the Crash! _____

- Today one out of two marriages ends in divorce.
- In a survey conducted by *Better Homes and Gardens* among 100,000 readers, 53 percent responded that a lack of commitment is the main reason that marriages fail, with 11 percent giving adultery as the major cause. Fifty-five percent point to divorce as the greatest threat to family life while 47 percent identify moral decay as the greatest threat.
- Psychiatrist Jean-Francois Saucier of the University of Montreal says that divorce has a more severe effect on a child's outlook than the death of a parent.
- In a recent Louis Harris survey of 1,000, nearly one-third of 12- to 17-year-old teens have lost their virginity, and 57 percent had sex by the time they reached 17.
- In just 30 years, births out of wedlock, as a percentage of all births, increased 450 percent.
- Twenty percent of all babies born are birthed to unwed mothers. This figure had climbed to a record high according to the National Center for Health Statistics.
- Since Roe vs. Wade decision in 1973 and up to 1988, 21 million babies have been aborted in the U.S.
- As of August 1984, 40,051 persons in the U.S. have acquired

AIDS according to the Center for Disease Control. Of this number 23,165 are known to have died.
- By the end of 1991, an estimated 270,000 cases of AIDS will have occurred with 179,000 deaths in the U.S. within the decade since the disease was first recognized, states a report by Surgeon General C. Everett Koop.

Based on the following:

C. Everett Koop, *The Surgeon General's Report on Acquired Immune Deficiency Syndrome* (U.S. Department of Health and Human Services, 1986), p. 6.

Centers for Disease Control, "Update: Acquired Immunodeficiency Syndrome—United States," *Morbidity and Mortality Weekly Report* (August 14, 1987).

Josh McDowell and Dick Day, *Why Wait?* (San Bernardino: Here's Life Publishers, 1987), pp. 35,36.

Kate Greer, "What's Happening to American Families?" *Better Homes and Gardens* November 1988, p. 34.

"News and Such," a column in *Focus on the Family* November 1986, p. 11, March 1987, p. 10, June 1989, p. 11, July 1988, p. 3.

By Margaret Rosenberger

13

Divorce: Is It an Option?

RICK BUNDSCHUH

Before you start to read this chapter, flip a coin. Call heads or tails before it lands. Perhaps you will call the toss correctly, perhaps you won't. But the odds that you will win this game are just about the same as the odds that you will win at marriage: 50/50. About half of the marriages entered into in the United States end in divorce. Unfortunately, being a Christian does not seem to improve divorce statistics dramatically.

DIVORCE AND CONTEMPORARY CULTURE

Something has gone wrong—desperately wrong. And whether we want to face it or not, in our culture, getting married and staying married to the same partner is pretty much a matter of chance.

This is not a pessimistic statement designed to douse the

hopes and dreams of people who are married or who desire to be married. It is a dose of realism so that we can be better prepared to give and keep one of the most sacred promises that a person can make.

Since humans began walking the earth, there has been marriage. But what marriage was then or even a hundred years ago is not what marriage is today. The modern, secular view of marriage likens it to a contract that can be amended or ended at a later date. To this contract the condition "as long as we both shall love" may replace the well-known phrase "as long as we both shall live." This implies that the couple agrees to share all things mutually until one or the other no longer wants to continue in the relationship. Then they simply file the proper documents in court, and they are let out of the contract much the same way that a person terminates a lease on a car or breaks with a business partner. They are then free to make another marriage contract with another person. This contract can be made as many times as they deem it necessary for their own personal happiness. While the marriage contract is in effect, faithfulness is expected. This form of marriage has been termed "serial monogamy."

To some, serial monogamy is seen as the natural consequence of increased life span. One marriage, they reason, might have worked in the days when the average life expectancy was 40. But when the average person lives to be 70, 75 or even 80, how can one spouse satisfy the needs of so many stages of life?

According to this way of thinking, property, friends and children are divided up between the two former lovers and everybody lives happily ever after. But people, especially children, don't subdivide as nicely as pieces of property.

Viewing marriage as a temporary contract has caused countless tales of misery. Many of you holding this book are among those whose lives have been disrupted by the chaos of divorce. Most people suffer when divorce touches their lives.

DIVORCE AND THE CHURCH

Divorce has become a difficult issue in the church. On one hand Christians have a strong tradition and biblical teaching that divorce is wrong. But on the other hand, their churches are filled with many people who have or will experience it.

The response of the Church to divorce has been wide and varied. In some circles it has been treated like it didn't exist. Clergy and congregations seem to stick their heads in the sand, ignoring it.

The other extreme is to heap blame on the suffering parties, effectively amputating from the Body of believers anyone who has been involved in a divorce. Other Christians have decided to "up-date" their view of divorce. They have essentially taken the position that the secular world has taken: Divorce is unpleasant, but things like that just happen.

Many Christians are still groping to find what they really feel is the right position on the subject to divorce. They are looking for clear guidelines on when divorce is permissible, how marriages can be risk-proofed, and how they should treat people who are divorced.

To begin to understand the issues surrounding divorce, we must first consider what marriage is all about and what role God and His Word play in it.

WHAT'S MARRIAGE

It has been said that no one gets married for the right reasons. There is a bit of truth in this statement. Some people get married to escape a bad home. Others marry in an attempt to find security. Still others may be forced to marry by an unwanted pregnancy. But most of these people are also getting married because they desire the companionship of the person they are marrying. They do not want to be alone.

Companionship is not a bad reason to marry. In fact it is the reason that God gave for creating Eve. "It is not good for the man to be alone," God said (Gen. 2:18). But Christian marriage involves more than two persons. The third Person in the relationship is God.

C. S. Lewis in his book *Mere Christianity* draws a definite distinction between a marriage involving God and one which is simply a civil ceremony. Lewis commented, "There ought to be two distinct kinds of marriage: one governed by the State with rules enforced on all citizens, the other governed by the Church with rules enforced by her on her own members. The distinction ought to be quite sharp, so that a man knows which couples are married in a Christian sense and which are not."[1]

Marriage in the eyes of Christians involves God not only because He is an integral part of our lives, but also because we believe that He designed marriage as a primary element of all society. We believe that marriage is His idea and therefore subject to His rules and guidelines. Because non-Christians do not acknowledge this basic concept, they cannot be expected to bring their lives into line with it.

Marriage in the eyes of Christians involves God not only because He is an integral part of our lives, but also because we believe that He designed marriage as a primary element of all society.

This fact is one of the main reasons why the Bible forbids those who believe in Christ to marry those who do not share the same faith (see 2 Cor. 6:14). A Christian who marries a non-Christian will start his or her married life on a faulty premise. The Christian at least professes to have lines, rules and margins that have been immovably set by an eternal God. The non-

Christian may start with a very similar set of ideas, but because his or her rules are only fixed by what seems to be best at the time, he or she can change the rules to fit wishes or moods without warning or even explanation. It is easy to see how this can affect the long-term quality of a relationship.

When one spouse becomes a believer after marriage, a whole new set of problems comes into play. In this instance the believer's ideas and standards will begin to change as God works in his or her life. The non-Christian partner may not approve of these changes and may feel short-changed, betrayed or even jealous. In such a relationship many questions need to be resolved. Is it okay to say grace? Attend Sunday and midweek services? Send the kids to Christian camp? How do two people with opposing world views hold together a relationship? What if the non-Christian objects? Is there a point where God no longer expects the Christian to keep the marriage vow?

DIVORCE AND THE BIBLE

Most Christians agree that this point is reached when an unbeliever no longer wants to live with or abandons his or her Christian spouse. This comes from a passage of Scripture written by the apostle Paul in which he apparently tried to remedy a tough situation in the early Church. This is what most likely happened: As the early Church grew, many people from households that once were completely pagan became believers. Suddenly one party or the other in a marriage was renouncing the old statutes of an erroneous religion and was embracing a new faith in Jesus. On many occasions this caused great disruptions in relationships. Christian wives or husbands sought relief from their marriages to unsaved spouses. In their old way of life, something this drastic would have been handled with a divorce. (Ancient Greek divorce decrees are preserved today and they are remarkably similar to the laws used in most courts today.) But Paul forbade divorce when the unbelieving mate consented to stay with the Christian. In fact, the Christian was told to make the best of the situation, to show love and respect and to provide a spiritual environment for the children of the marriage. But, Paul said, if the non-Christian wanted out, divorce was a permissible option (see 1 Cor. 7:12-16).

The Bible says that there is another situation in which a person may divorce his or her mate. Jesus gave this instruction in Matthew 19:3-11.

Some Pharisees came to Jesus to test Him. They asked, "Is it lawful for a man to divorce his wife for any and every reason?" (v. 3). These men were probably trying to draw Jesus in on one side of an argument that was being waged between opposing groups of Jewish teachers. Some taught that divorce was no big deal and allowed it freely. Others held to a much more narrow view.

Jesus sided with the latter. He clarified the situation by saying: "Haven't you read . . . that at the beginning the Creator 'made them male and female,' and said, 'For this reason a man will leave his father and mother and be united to his wife, and the two will become one flesh'? So they are no longer two, but one. Therefore what God has joined together, let man not separate."

"'Why then,' [the Pharisees] asked, 'did Moses command that a man give his wife a certificate of divorce and send her away?'

"Jesus replied, 'Moses permitted you to divorce your wives because your hearts were hard. But it was not this way from the beginning. I tell you that anyone who divorces his wife, except for marital unfaithfulness, and marries another woman commits adultery'" (vv. 4-9).

When the disciples heard Christ's stern requirements, they recognized the seriousness of the commitment and questioned aloud the wisdom of marriage: "If this is the situation between a husband and a wife, it is better not to marry" (v. 10).

Jesus pointed out, "Not everyone can accept this teaching,

but only those to whom it has been given" (v. 11). In other words, marriage is so serious that we need to approach it with the highest degree of personal integrity.

Clearly Jesus allowed divorce in the case of adultery. The Greek word *porneia*, from which we get the word pornography and which is translated in this passage "marital unfaithfulness," means not just sex with a person other than your mate, but also includes other sexual sins such as homosexuality and incest. Jesus taught that sexual sin was grounds for divorce.

The concept of divorce *is* biblical. As Jay Adams says in his excellent book on the subject, "Let us be clear about the fact that neither is the Bible silent on the subject of divorce, nor does it always, under all circumstances, for everyone, condemn divorce .... It is altogether true that God hates divorce. But He neither hates all divorces in the same way nor hates every aspect of divorce. He hates what occasions *every* divorce."[2]

Quite clearly the Bible authorizes divorce but at the same time does so in a very limited context. The real spirit of the Scripture leads believers to strive for reconciliation. The primary call for the Christian in a troubled marriage is to forgive the wrongs of the person he or she married, not to use these wrongs as an excuse to change partners. Even major wrongs such as adultery can be healed with the work of the Holy Spirit and the effort of both parties.

The Bible is silent about many other reasons that people have for divorce. Obviously physical violence or mistreatment are reasons to separate, but again, the objective should be the cure of the problem, not divorce.

When God created marriage He created it to be permanent—lasting for the lives of the two lovers. Jesus declared, "What God has joined together let man not separate" (Matt. 19:6). Modern standards have come a long way in perverting God's design with trendy thinking and disposable relationships. But what steps can we take to avoid divorce?

For one thing, each Christian must not enter into the marriage relationship lightly. Before we make that permanent commitment we should ask ourselves questions such as these:

- Would I stick by my lover if he (she) had a serious illness that left him (her) confined to a wheelchair or bed for life?
- Would I look elsewhere if that handsome (pretty) face became deformed through disease or a horrible accident?
- Would I weather mental illness, the death of a child, unemployment and bill collectors without seeking greener pastures?
- Would I stick with him (her) after time and gravity have taken their toll? Or would I be tempted to trade him (her) in on a new model?
- Is my desire to marry based on the love, companionship and respect I feel for my beloved, or on something else?
- Have we discussed the important issues of faith, children and what we will expect of each other in the marriage?

Real marriage involves real everyday issues. It is not a white horse, prince and castle. It is lots of fun, but it is also lots of work.

Real marriage involves real everyday issues. It is not a white horse, prince and castle. It is lots of fun, but it is also lots of work.

Marriage is a sacred promise made before God. The marriage ceremony is almost always seen as a joyous occasion where the bride and groom want to share their happiness with friends and family. That is why weddings are among the most common celebrations in all cultures.

As Christians, we are asked to obey the laws of the land in which we live. That is why we not only hold a religious ceremony, but also complete the civil obligations of marriage such as taking out a marriage license and having blood tests.

But what happens after the marriage?

COPING WITH CONFLICT

Christian marriage specialist Norm Wright believes that communication is the most important ingredient in a healthy marriage. And he offers the following ten tips for dealing with conflict:

1. Don't avoid conflict with the silent treatment.
2. Don't save "emotional trading stamps" [hold grudges].
3. If possible, prepare the setting for disagreement.
4. Attack the problem, not each other . . .
   . . . back up accusations with facts
   . . . remember to forget
   . . . no cracks about in-laws or relatives
   . . . no cracks about your mate's appearance
   . . . no dramatics.
5. Don't throw your feelings like stones.
6. Stay on the subject.
7. Offer solutions with your criticisms.
8. Never say, "you never . . . . "
9. Don't manipulate your mate with, "It's all *my* fault."
10. Be humble—you could be wrong.[3]

More serious steps must be taken in marriages where substance or physical abuse, infidelity or compulsive behavior are involved. These situations need professional attention.

Because marriage is an act that involves God, when there are problems in a marriage, the Church should offer guidance and help.

For this reason, some churches have opened Christian counseling centers. Others offer support groups for members struggling through marriage conflicts, or who are broken-hearted because of divorce. There are ministries to the children of broken homes and agencies that try to bring about reconciliation.

One area where many Christians find it difficult to act, however, is in the area of church discipline. When adultery is the basis for the divorce of fellow believers, how should the Church respond to the adulterer? What if the adulterer is a personal friend?

Loving confrontations may turn a friend around. Intervention in Christ's name often brings new hope, especially when family, close friends and church unite in their actions. A personal appeal to return to Christ and biblical living makes a powerful impact. Some will respond well to a personal appeal; others will not. Some will return to Christ, and their marriage will be restored; others will not. Whatever the outcome the Christian who is spiritual will want to try to be a part of the restoration process (see Jas. 5:19-20).[4]

Sadly, often all efforts for reconciliation and counsel fail and divorce results. What hope is there for the Christian in this situation?

RESTORATION

For one thing, divorced Christians can be encouraged that God is forgiving. Even Christians who are not the "guilty party" may feel burdened by the mistakes they made in their marriages. They may be unnecessarily carrying a load of self-blame. But God wants to "purify us from all unrighteousness" (1 John 1:9). This act of purification is a necessary step in preparing to move on. If God restored David, who had sung Psalm 23 before committing adultery, He is also willing to restore the Christian who is divorced. Divorce is not the unpardonable sin.

In relating to divorced Christians, the Church must imitate

Jesus: what He said and did; and how He behaved toward people. Although Jesus gave strict guidelines for divorce, He also showed love and acceptance to sinners who were considered outcasts by society (see Matt. 9:10-13; 8:1-11). Christians need to help their divorced brothers and sisters cope with the difficult problems that accompany divorce. They need to help them towards restoration and healing.

But what about the divorced person who wants to remarry?

REMARRIAGE

Different groups of Christians have different responses to Christians who divorce and remarry. Some accept fully into fellowship those who were divorced before their conversion or who had biblical grounds for divorce. Others accept into fellowship, but not leadership, such believers. Some churches do not put any restrictions on the participation of divorced and remarried members as long as the second marriage is not to a person they became involved with during their first marriage. Still others will not permit remarriage under any circumstances.

None of these responses is perfect. It is difficult to balance the need to emphasize the seriousness of breaking the marriage commitment with the need to minister to those who are broken by divorce. But difficult as it may be, the Church is called to respond as Christ's Body in the world. In achieving balance the Church can be encouraged by nothing less than the character of God who is at once righteous, holy, pure, compassionate and merciful.

Notes

1. C. S. Lewis, *Mere Christianity* (New York: Macmillan Publishing Co., 1952), p. 87.

2. Jay E. Adams, *Marriage, Divorce and Remarriage in the Bible* (Grand Rapids: Zondervan Publishing House, 1980), p. 23.
3. H. Norman Wright, *Communication: Key to Your Marriage* (Ventura: Regal Books, 1974), p. 157.
4. Charles Mylander, *Running the Red Lights* (Ventura: Regal Books, 1986), pp. 116,117.

14

Roles: Manliness and Womanliness

RICK BUNDSCHUH

If you've ever gone fishing you probably have had the experience of getting your line so tangled that it resembles a filament bird's nest. Sometimes the tangle comes from casting your line incorrectly. Sometimes it comes from careless handling. But once fouled, the job of unraveling it is one that takes careful concentration. It may involve a great deal of frustration as well. In fact, a lot of times just when you think you have all the knots out, another one pops up and dares you to be finished with the job. Many people get so annoyed that they simply cut the line rather than hassle with it.

Trying to sort out the roles that men and women should have in today's society, especially any roles that are addressed by Scripture, is much like trying to untangle fishing line. It takes concentration to undo the mix-up, the effort may prove frustrating, and the answers may be elusive.

The very first thing we must understand is that many of the roles that people consider to be traditional are not very old at all. At the same time, some of the distinctly masculine or feminine parts played in society have never changed throughout history and are not likely to change at any time soon.

For example, a role that is unchanging is that of childbearing. God specifically designed women's bodies for this function. Also women are more involved with early care and feeding of babies. Although contemporary men may become very involved with their young children due to their own desire or social urging, women will most likely remain the basic nurturers. Again, God has specially equipped them for this purpose (see Titus 2:5).

Trying to sort out the roles that men and women should have in today's society, especially any roles that are addressed by Scripture, is much like trying to untangle fishing line.

Roles that are dictated by the way we were created are called *natural* roles. Most people assume that the way things are "supposed to be" is for men and women to be functioning in their natural roles. This attitude is based on common sense and recognition of the obvious differences between men and women.

There are other roles that we may think of as being natural roles but which really are more modern traditions. Many people feel that men have always gone off to work outside the home for hours while Mom stayed home to wash the clothes, prepare the food and raise the kids. We have come to think of these functions as being the duties that are natural for men and women. Yet they are really the inventions of a more modern era.

A short review of history may help to unravel some of the

knots in the tangle of what we consider to be the roles of men and women.

LOOKING BACK

For thousands of years men and women shared responsibility for the same thing: survival. From early civilization until the industrial revolution, most people lived, worked and died trying to force enough produce out of the ground to feed their families, satisfy their landlords and make a little money for meager purchases. Mom and Dad both were involved in the care and tending of crops, animals and land. Not only Mom and Dad, but also every child born into the family had to lend a hand in some very hard work almost as soon as he or she could walk. The whole family pulled together.

Life in the cities of this era was organized similarly. If Dad was a woodcarver, he set up shop in the front of the house and the family lived in the back of the house. Everybody got involved in some aspect of the woodcarving business. All members of the family shared in the everyday household duties. Although Mom probably was more concerned with food preparation and Dad more with cutting wood, chores involving the small garden patch and the making of clothing were probably shared. Children received instructions and care from both parents.

Throughout most of history, farmers' children grew up to be farmers and woodcarvers' children grew up to be woodcarvers. Members of the family were stuck with each other all day long as they labored for their survival.

The kings, queens and other nobility of the period were the exceptions to this pattern. They were the privileged few who had enough money and power to escape the toil.

Then after thousands of years of this routine, a dramatic earthquake of change shook up civilization. Although simple machinery had always existed, a period of great emphasis upon mechanic inventions began. Machines became much more common and more complicated. Labor systems changed to facilitate their use. The industrial revolution was ushered in.

Factories popped up everywhere. In increasing numbers men left their home industries and fields and trudged off to work in factories or in the coal mines that supplied the fuel for the factories. Men who had once painstakingly carved furniture by hand began manufacturing it on newfangled machines. Those who had carded wool for the family's clothes while sitting by the fireplace at home began laboring in mills over great spindles of thread.

Since abstinence was the only form of birth control, most families were large. As the fathers left home to work, mothers had little choice but to stay home and raise the kids. (Although in the poorest families, the mothers and children were also forced to work in mines, factories and mills.)

The world became more efficient, regimented and streamlined as time went on. Child labor was abolished. Workdays were cut from 12 to 16 hours a day to 8. Vacations, unknown to previous generations, were invented. More and more of a man's self-esteem became connected with the workplace. More and more of a woman's self-worth came from raising her children well and being a good housekeeper.

The world of Wally, the Beaver, June and Ward Cleaver evolved. Dad went to the office more often than the factory now, and Mom cared for the house and kids. Her leisure time was spent playing bridge or doing volunteer work. It appeared as though everything was going smoothly until one day the roles for men and women came under the scrutiny of some very dissatisfied women. The Women's Movement had begun. But this did not happen overnight. Nor did industrial revolution proceed at a steady rate in relation to how it affected the roles of men and women. There were ebbs and flows in the course of history. The various duties of men and women switched hands again and again. Women's rights movements gained or lost ground.

CHANGES

An example of how roles changed can be seen in the history of the twentieth century. During the first and second world wars men left their homes to fight on foreign soil. Their absence in industry, along with the acute need for equipment to fight the wars, put women into the foundries, steel mills and munitions' factories. Women occupied jobs that a few years before they would have thought to be the sole role of men. But when the men returned from war, the women returned to their homes and their previous roles in society.

But in the second half of the twentieth century a couple of new elements were added to the social brew. These factors would forever affect how women viewed themselves and their roles in society. One of these elements was the invention of the birth control pill. It was effective, easy to use and could be controlled by the woman. For the first time in history women could control how many (if any) children they would have and when these children would be born. The size of families shifted from large to small. Also at the same time, the life spans of both men and women lengthened, and children left home at an earlier age. This left many women, whose primary job had been mothering, with decades of time on their hands.

For many women it was as if chains around their legs had been snapped and they had sprouted wings. Careers outside the home became more of a reality. Although there had always been women who seriously sought an education in order to pursue a profession, they had been in the minority. Usually it was only upper-middle-class or middle-class women who went on to college. Often they were just biding their time between high school and marriage. Now, however, women flocked to colleges to prepare for careers.

Women also flooded the workplace in jobs that did not require college preparation.

The feminist movement encouraged women to examine their functions in society and to change the roles they had traditionally filled. Women went to court to challenge the right of employers to keep them out of certain positions that were filled by males only.

But women were not the only ones who were affected by these changes. For generations men had seen themselves in the roles of providers for the family. They were the hunters, the breadwinners, the guys who literally brought home the bacon. As women pressed for equal pay and even more for equal worth, men began to wonder what their roles really were. Men struggled to decide if they should try to be the rough guy loner portrayed by movie heroes or enroll in home economics classes. They wondered if they should open the car door for their dates or if they would be considered chauvinists for trying to have good manners. What should they call women who didn't like to be called miss, missus or girl? The reel that had held the threads of what it meant to be a man or a women was set spinning. As the threads came off the reel, they became more and more mixed up and tangled.

Into this confusion another interesting factor has been added: the computer. Many futurists see a return to home industry being prompted by the computer. In increasing numbers, people will no longer have to go to an office to work. Instead they can work in their homes and can hook up by telephone to the central computer systems of their companies. People will be free to work at various hours of the day and night instead of being constrained by a schedule. This could very well reshuffle the roles of men and women once again. If the man spends all day at home plunking on the keys of a computer, or if he can create his own hours, he will be more free to help raise the children. What other changes may come about we can only guess. But the changes that will come through the computer will probably be more significant than the changes brought about by the industrial revolution.

It is into this confusion about sexual roles that most of us were born or grew up. The chaos of voices, feelings, emotions, expectations, traditions and ideas has both men and women wandering around in a vast twilight zone, searching for a role in life that will make sense to them. People need to feel that there are some things that don't change. For these things they often look to the Bible.

Some traditionalists like to point out verses of Scripture that show women fulfilling the duties of food preparation, house cleaning and the rest to support the view that these duties are ordained by God. People on the other side of the argument like to point out that these passages simply reflected the culture that was in existence at the time. They were not necessarily prescriptions for women's roles in all societies that were to follow.

The Bible is clear on the concept of the equality of men and women. This is the first knot in the tangle of defining roles that must be undone. But being equal is not being the same. Men and women think, act, feel and perform tasks differently. There are very distinct differences in their physical strength: While man have more power, women have greater ability to endure. While these traits are general (you may find some women are stronger than some men, or some men are more sensitive to the emotions of others than some women), they are consistent throughout society.

To suggest that men and women are the same is silly. But they are equal in the sense that while different, they have the same basic worth or value. When we understand this idea, we've untangled one knot.

We all know that there are differences in male and female hormones, but studies indicate that hormones dictate more than who gets breasts and who gets to shave their faces. Two women psychologists found that females who had been exposed to male hormones during a certain time of brain development in the womb wound up with typically masculine personality traits such as aggressiveness and initiative.[1]

But there are a myriad of questions that still need to be sorted out. Should women be allowed to have the same jobs as men? Should women be eligible for the draft? What roles should a man assume? What roles should be left primarily to women?

Few people would argue that there is comfort in men and women having different roles. A clear example of this is in dating customs. Most women still want to have the door opened for them, help with putting on their coats and for the man to pick up the tab for the evening out. Imagine the surpise on a man's face if his date opened all the doors for him, or her expression if he presented her with the bill for a meal at an expensive restaurant! Dating can be difficult enough with some established roles and rules. Most people like having guidelines.

Dating roles are not the only ones that society dictates. There are other roles that men naturally gravitate towards as an expression of their masculinity. Likewise, women seem to get a feeling of satisfaction from roles that are considered feminine. Interestingly, these positions often have little to do with maleness or femaleness and everything to do with how the culture defines masculinity and feminity. For example, in the Soviet Union most doctors are women—a reversal of the way it is in the United States. So in that country becoming a doctor is considered something that women are most likely to strive for. Men enter into what would be, for Soviets, more manly fields of work. Now we all know that men and women are equally qualified to be doctors, but in the Soviet Union society has tinted the role of doctor a feminine pink while in the United States it is macho blue.

We can untie another of the snarls in understanding sex roles when we see that oftentimes the way men and women function in society is purely dictated by the culture and not by any real differences in them as persons. Cultures pronounce some roles as masculine and some as feminine. There are always those who cross these culturally-defined lines with no problem—pro football players who enjoy needlepoint or women who enjoy racing cars. But dabbling too much in the opposite sex's role is usually viewed with suspicion.

Sometimes culturally determined roles change. It no longer seems strange to have male telephone operators or women letter carriers. Not too long ago the title telephone operator was solely a woman's title and letter carriers and postal workers were called mailmen or postmen.

Sometimes changes in sexual roles are brought about by circumstances. A single father may find himself fighting his way through the business world with the *Wall Street Journal* in hand during the day while spending time with *Betty Crocker's Cookbook* at night. He may have to develop not only the skills necessary to perform his daytime job, but also expertise with an iron.

One more knot is untangled when we realize that a person does not give up his masculinity or her femininity by crossing the role boundaries here and there.

In some ways, however, society is very resistant to change. Even in homes where equality is emphasized, there have been marked returns to what is considered more traditional arrangements with men resuming the roles of providers and women returning to the roles of nurturers. One researcher points out that it is usually the woman who initiates the return to the traditional arrangement.[2] This seems to be a very recent development of a backlash to the feminist movement. Many women long to return to simpler days.

SIMPLIFYING THE CONFUSION

The Bible gives some help in defining the roles men and women are called to by God. In 1 Timothy 5:8 the apostle Paul gave a stinging rebuke to men who professed to be believers but who neglected to provide for their families: "If anyone does not provide for his relatives, and especially for his immediate family, he has denied the faith and is worse than an unbeliever." In this passage and in numerous examples of men in Scripture, we see that men have the responsibilities of being providers for their loved ones. This clearly fits not only with historic roles that men have assumed, but also with the current realities of our society.

For both men and women there are plenty of ways to be comfortable in manhood or womanhood and still be the kinds of persons that God created us to be!

The Bible does not suggest that women sit passively at home waiting to cook up the vittles. Scripture suggests that women be productive as well. In the famous passage on the characteristics of a noble or virtuous woman, Proverbs 31, we find a woman engaged in real estate transactions and business endeavors that turn a profit. She demonstrates managerial skills as well as benevolence to the poor, caring for the family and serving the Lord. It is important to note that her husband is considered blessed by his peers because he has such an industrious wife (see v. 31). Obviously neither one of them were threatened by the success of the other. This is a good a model for today as it was for yesterday.

Biblical roles are suggested in marriage as well. But careful study of these roles and the passages will lead one to conclude that the message is more about "loveship" than it is about "lordship."

With all the pressures for men to be macho men and for women to be superwomen, it is easy to get lost in the tangle of roles. The simplest thing to be in that case is the person you are. If you are a man who enjoys cooking a meal once in a while, don't hide it. It you are a woman who is fascinated by the workings of mechanical things, go ahead and get your hands greasy. Trying to be something that you are not is a great waste of time and generally a big disappointment as well. Fortunately, for both men and women there are plenty of ways to be comfortable in manhood or womanhood and still be the kinds of persons that God created us to be!

As the line defining masculinity and feminity untangles, we will undoubtedly come to the following conclusions:

- Men and women are uniquely different and skilled in various areas. They usually are most comfortable when they are operating within their own unique realms.
- Men and women have the same basic worth as individuals. One is not superior to the other.
- Some roles often shift back and forth between men and women depending on their cultures, economics and other conditions.
- Roles for men and women come from natural, God-given sources as well as from societal and upbringing environments.
- Enjoying some of the activities usually thought of as being the role of the opposite sex is not necessarily a reflection on one's masculinity or femininity.
- Being who you are is the most important role you will have to play.

Notes

1. Peter and Evelyn Blitchington, *Understanding the Male Ego* (Nashville: Thomas Nelson Publishers, 1984), p. 28.
2. Ibid., p. 27.

15

Women and the Church: Shared Leadership or Male Headship?

ANNETTE PARRISH

Outside a cold, gray rain steadily pelted the windows. But inside the church sanctuary it seemed warm. Fourteen-year-old Amy closed her eyes as she listened to the words of the worship choruses. It was the first Sunday of the month and in this medium-sized California church, that meant communion would be shared in the morning service.

Communion Sunday always affected Amy positively. She felt the comfort that comes from being a part of a body of believers. She was awed by participating in a symbolic meal that had been shared in unbroken history by millions of believers since Jesus first shared it with His disciples.

As the pastor asked the 12 elders to come forward to distribute the bread, Amy opened her eyes. For the first time something invaded upon her peaceful reflections. Amy felt as though she had been struck across her face. Her cheeks flushing with resentment, she turned to her mother and said, "Why are the elders all men?"

Meanwhile in a different building in the same town another group of Christians gathered to worship. Stepping to the pulpit, Bible in hand, the pastor looked out at the congregation. The church had grown. Esther opened the Bible and began her sermon.

Halfway across the United States a visiting woman missionary from the Philippines was startled when several churches would not allow her to share the pulpit with her husband. She was told by the senior pastor at one of these churches that his flock strictly follows the biblical instruction, "Women should remain silent in church" (1 Cor. 14:34). Having been raised in China where her mother preached to Chinese congregations and having served in the Philippines where she often took the pulpit, Kari was very perplexed. She was even further bewildered when she attended some women's ministries functions where color analysis (figuring out which clothing colors are the most flattering), cooking and the home arts seemed to be more important than a Bible study.

While it is true that women's ministries in most churches include Bible studies, it is not, however, the norm for men's ministries to offer the same smorgasbord of classes and activities. In the majority of today's churches, men are offered solely in-depth Bible studies with an occasional course on money management. Classes in gardening, automotive repairs and how to organize your garage are not on the schedule.

The issue of how women should serve was also confronting Pastor Norris. He had just come out of one of the most disturbing church board meetings of his long career. It all had to do with hiring an associate pastor. A very capable woman had applied for the job and although in his denomination the local church was empowered to ordain and hire women, his congregation was split on whether it would be right. In the board meeting sincere Christians with solid Bible backgrounds had hotly debated scriptural teaching regarding women in the Church. To make matters worse, this group of believers seemed to be focusing on the controversy instead of on their unity in Christ and how they should be serving Him in the community. But who was right? Pastor Norris retired to his office to spend long hours praying and studying Scriptures relating to the issue.

Jesus demonstrated a radical departure from the culture of His day. He praised the faith of women.

The controversy surrounding how women should serve the Church can be confusing. Bible scholars differ on how key verses dealing with women should be interpreted. Cultural standards and church tradition seem to further complicate the issue. Some see women pushing for more involvement in the Church to be a result of the feminist movement. Others see the effort to keep women out of certain positions as a backlash against the same movement. But this issue did not originate in the twentieth century. In fact, its roots go back many, many centuries.

SOME HISTORY

Although the Old Testament records that Israel had women rulers (Deborah—see Judg. 4:4; Athaliah—see 2 Kings 11:3) and women prophets (Miriam—see Exod. 15:20; Deborah—see Judg. 4:4; Huldah—see 2 Kings 22:14), the culture in which Jesus ministered in the first century was one that openly discriminated against women. Many Pharisees started their day with a prayer that went something like this: "I thank God that I was not born a slave, a Gentile or a woman."

Ancestry was recorded through the fathers (check out the

"begets" in the Bible). Crowds were counted according to how many men were present; women and children were not taken into account (see John 6:10).

Jesus demonstrated a radical departure from the culture of His day. He praised the faith of women. He allowed Mary, the sister of Martha, to sit at His feet, a place of honor, while He taught (see Luke 10:39). Jesus seemed to assume that women were capable not only of learning and understanding but also of engaging in debate.[1] Many women, including Mary Magdalene, Joanna and Susanna, traveled with Jesus and His disciples, supporting them with their own funds and listening while Jesus preached.

After Jesus returned to heaven, women retained their improved position for a while. Although the structure of society had not changed, attitudes within the body of believers had.

Women attended early church gatherings with their husbands and children. They prophesied in these meetings. They participated in communion. And, they suffered martyrdom along with their Christian brothers.

Women were also allowed certain roles in the leadership of the Church in the first and second centuries. It is likely that women, such as Phoebe, held the position of deacon (see Rom. 16:1,2)[2]. There is a difference of opinion in church circles as to whether women were excluded from the offices of elder and pastor. The majority of church groups believe women did not hold these offices. However, some believe that under certain conditions they did. They cite the example of a woman named Junias (see Rom. 16:7), who may have been an apostle (a highly controversial position if held by a woman), and historical evidence such as the discovery of a wall painting in the catacombs of Rome that pictures seven women distributing communion, a duty performed by pastors and elders.

Bible scholars also differ as to whether the instruction, "I do not permit a woman to teach" (1 Tim. 2:12) was directed by the apostle Paul to certain churches or to all churches and for all time. Some interpret this instruction as meaning that women can teach children and other women, but not men. But it is evident that one woman, a close friend of the apostle Paul named Priscilla, taught Apollos—an important man in the early church (see Acts 18:24-26). It may be important to note that Priscilla taught Apollos in her home, not at a church gathering. Although Priscilla's husband, Aquila, shared in the teaching of Apollos, some people believe that because Priscilla's name is listed first in verse 26, she held the leading position in the teaching process.

Slowly, as the years passed, women began to lose ground. As the Church grew, their meetings became more formal. Gatherings that had been characterized by sharing, prayer, singing of hymns and prophesying began to follow certain forms called liturgies. Men who served as pastors, and who had always taught and shepherded groups of Christians became recognized as *the* leaders of specific congregations. Pastors began to lead the church services, reading from the Scriptures and teaching what the Scriptures meant. Prophesying, a ministry in which women had been allowed to participate, became uncommon.[3]

Congregations were organized into larger groups and headed by men called bishops. As the hierarchal system grew, more offices were added: archbishop, cardinal, pope. Women did not serve in these offices.

However, with the changing church structure, certain new positions did open to women. Around the fourth century, retreats, which we now call convents, opened. Women who renounced the normal life of marrying and caring for a family could go to these retreats and dedicate their lives to prayer and charitable works. At around the same time, similar retreats that would come to be known as monasteries opened for men.

Women and men from these retreats communicated and joined together in projects to further God's Kingdom. Notably, Jerome, who first translated the Bible into a language that the average person of the day could understand (the Vulgate), said he profited in his work from the criticism and questioning of Marcella, a Christian woman who understood Greek and Hebrew and whose home had become a center for prayer and study.

Events in history gave the monasteries and converts another important role. As the years rolled by, Rome lost power. Barbarian hordes invaded cities, ravaging and burning everything in their path. Much of the literature of the early Church, and many of the oldest copies of Scripture survived the pillage because the works were hidden by dedicated Christians in convents and monasteries.

As women lost ground socially throughout the Dark Ages and the Middle Ages, they also lost position and respect in the Church.

By the fifth century, tribes of barbarians were invading Rome itself. Often Christian women were carried off as hostages or captives. Much of the evangelization of Northern Europe was done by these women witnessing to their captor husbands.

But as women lost ground socially throughout the Dark Ages and the Middle Ages, they also lost position and respect in the Church. When as a result of the Reformation, monasteries and convents were abolished in Protestant denominations, women no longer had an office in which they could serve. They entered into a period of powerlessness and dishonor that would last for many years. The situation was so bad that an English pastor, John Donne, raised quite a controversy by proposing that it might be possible in rare instances that a few women could have a few virtues. It is even more outrageous that another of Donne's proposals was considered controversial in the 1600s: Donne believed that women possessed souls.

Into this atmosphere of repression came a glimmer of hope. The Bible was being translated into languages that common people understood. This had not been done since the fourth century when Jerome translated it into the Vulgate.

In 1611 the King James Bible became available to English-speaking people. Christians who hungered to read God's Word began earnest Bible study. One of these Christians was George Fox, the founder of the Quakers. The truths of the Bible led Fox to new understanding of what it means to be a Christian. Along with other unwelcome ideas, Fox's group of Christians believed in the "priesthood of all believers." Women were allowed to speak in church meetings. But this innovation was not well received. George Fox and many of his followers were often imprisoned or whipped. Some Quakers were executed both in England and in the United States.

In the 1700s a great revival that would influence the role of women in the Church began in England and the United States. John Wesley, founder of the Methodist Church, was one of the leaders of this movement that encouraged Bible reading, prayer and repentance of sins. Wesley appointed women as itinerant preachers, at first limiting them to five-minute talks, then gradually increasing the time they were allowed to speak. This trend of allowing women to speak in church continued with the Holiness Movement of the 1800s. Outstanding among women preachers during this period was Catherine Booth, co-founder of the Salvation Army.

Also in the 1800s, Christian women united with other women in two great political movements: one, to abolish slavery, and the other, to gain the right of women to vote. Both of these movements got strong support from some Christians and bitter opposition from others.

The brakes began to be applied to women's increased involvement in the Church in the 1920s. Churches of the Methodist and Holiness Movements had become very well established in society. They became more structured, and with this structure came the desire of church members to be led not by itinerate preachers, but by pastors who had attended seminary. Since most families sent only their sons to institutes of higher learning, and since most seminaries did not admit women, pulpits began to close to women.[4]

STATUS REPORT

Today different denominations or congregations take different positions on how women should serve the Church. These positions fall into three basic patterns.

Those who maintain that men alone were ordained by God to govern the Church hold to the view of *hierarchism*. These Christians base this view on New Testament Scriptures (1 Cor. 11:3; 12:12,13; 14:26-40; 1 Tim. 2:11-14) and on something called the creation ordinance.[5] The creation ordinance has four basic arguments taken from Genesis 2 which are used to show the subordination of women to men:

1. Woman was created after the man and is therefore secondary to him.
2. Woman was "taken from the man" and therefore secondary to him.
3. Woman was named by man and is therefore subordinate to him.
4. Woman was created to be a "helper" for man and as such is subordinate to him.

But in recent years many evangelical scholars have rejected all or part of the hierarchal position. Some of these Christians take the position that Scripture is better interpreted by a model that stresses partnership between men and women. They do not see the Genesis account as ordaining women to be forever subordinate to men.

Christians who hold this *egalitarian* position usually believe that when God said to Eve, "Your desire will be for your husband and he will rule over you" (Gen. 3:16), He was predicting a result of the Fall and was not setting in motion a model He ordained. They answer the four arguments of the creation ordinance with explanations similar to these:

1. Being created first does not imply superiority since frogs, cows and fish were all created before Adam.
2. Eve being taken from Adam stresses their unity/relatedness.[6]
3. In the original language the word translated "called" (Gen. 2:23) does not imply authority. It is different from the Hebrew word for "named" or "called" that is used when Adam named the animals. The word used in conjunction with Adam naming Eve does not imply Adam's authority.
4. The word translated as "helper" (Gen. 2:18) is used nineteen times in the Old Testament. Fifteen times it is used to describe God. So the word "helper" itself cannot imply inferiority or subordination.[7]

Many of the Christians who hold the position that the model for the Church is shared leadership believe that the apostle Paul's instructions for women to be silent in church were directed at specific situations in a few churches of the first century. They point out that historical tradition did not totally exclude women since, as previously mentioned, Israel had had women rulers and women prophets. Prophetesses in New Testament times included Anna (see Luke 2:36) and the four daughters of Philip (see Acts 21:8,9). These Christians feel that the overriding principle of equality in Christ (see Gal. 3:26-29) deserves more stress than patterns of church structure that can be interpreted from the original Greek to mean different things.

A growing number of Christians' viewpoints fall somewhere between the hierarchal and egalitarian models. Most mainstream Protestant churches would fit in this third category. Although 80 percent of these churches do not prohibit the ordination of women, they overwhelmingly, by denominational policy or simply by practice, are led by male senior pastors. Women are increasingly visible in other positions.

Christians in this middle ground stress that there are many different opportunities for serving in the Body and that these functions are equal in honor (see Rom. 12:5, 1 Cor. 12:5,6). In positions of authority women are most likely to be found as directors of Christian education, on mission boards, or teaching Sunday School. They may also serve as deaconesses. Less frequently they are seen in the roles of elder or pastor.

WHAT SHOULD WE DO?

Every Christian should consider the issue of how women should serve the Church. (That women should serve in some capacity is not in question.) A primary concern in looking into this issue must be sound biblical interpretation. Two basic questions need to be asked of every passage studied:

1. What was God saying through His human servant to the first hearers or readers of the message?
2. How should we understand and apply the passage to people today?

To answer the second of these questions, readers must understand that most of the teaching and commands in the Bible fall into one of the following two categories:

1. Unchanging highest ideals, norms, or standards;
2. Regulations for people where they were.

Keeping in mind these guidelines, there are several important questions that need to be examined in light of Scripture:

- Should women be allowed to preach and teach in church? What limitations, if any, should be applied to their preaching and teaching?
- What offices should be open to women? What is the scriptural basis for this position?
- How has society affected Christians' views on this topic?
- What should be the motivation for leadership?

While the issue of *how* women should serve is very important, it is more important that all Christians *continue to serve the Lord with a spirit of joy.* It is the Christian's privilege to know that God is perfectly just and loving in His dealings with His people. This includes how He desires each Christian, male or female, to serve Him. As His instruments on earth, we must reflect Him by submitting to His will and to each other. In doing this we can better demonstrate His love to each other and to a hurting world.

Notes

1. Mary Evans, *Women in the Bible* (Downers Grove: InterVarsity Press, 1983), p. 51.
2. Alvera and Berkeley Mickelsen, "What Happens to God's Gifts?" *The Standard,* May 1984, p. 37.
3. Kari Torjesen Malcolm, *Women at the Crossroads* (Downers Grove: InterVarsity Press, 1982), p. 93-95.
4. Ibid., pp. 119-133.
5. John Piper, "How Should a Woman Lead?" *The Standard,* May 1984, p. 34.
6. Francis A. Schaeffer, *Genesis in Space & Time* (Downers Grove: InterVarsity Press, 1972), pp. 46,47.
7. Evans, *Women in the Bible,* p. 16.

Some Scriptures to Study _____

Luke 10:38-42—In this passage Jesus affirmed that women should put Him first, before all other concerns.

Romans 16:1-3,6,7,12—These verses mention women who served the early Church.

1 Corinthians 11:3-16—Women are instructed to cover their heads in worship services. Some interpreters feel that this is a sign of submission that is still valid. Others say that it is a sign of a woman's own authority and relationship with God.

1 Corinthians 12:12,13—All Christians are equal in Christ and have a unique role in His Body.

1 Corinthians 14:26-40 and 1 Timothy 2:11-15—These passages are usually interpreted one of two ways: (1) Women should not preach or teach in public services or (2) This verse was a specific instruction to a particular situation where women were being disruptive.

Galatians 3:26-29—Another passage that stresses the believers' unity in Christ.

Ephesians 5:21-33—This passage describes God's plan for Christian marriage. Although both husbands and wives are told to submit to each other, the husband is in the position of authority.

1 Timothy 3:1-13—This passage describes the qualifications required of elders and deacons.

Recent Action: Women in Ministry _____

Episcopal Church
The Eastern Massachusetts diocese of the Episcopal church— largest diocese in the Unites States—elected on September 24, 1988, the first woman bishop in the history of the church, reports the Ventura County (Calif.) *Star-Free Press*. A black

priest at Philadelphia, Pennsylvania's Church of the Advocate, Barbara C. Harris, 58, was elected suffragan, or assistant bishop.

The Episcopal church is increasingly nominating women for bishop, but until Priest Harris's election to this office, none had won election.

Roman Catholic Church

According to the *Associated Press*, Pope John Paul II recently completed work on a major document, titled "Dignity of Women," that calls for more respect for women. The document, however, continues to uphold a Roman Catholic ban on women priests.

The announcement of the completion of this major document came in response to a worldwide bishops' synod that condemned sexual discrimination. Vatican officials acknowledged that the new statement will disappoint some women.

The Surgeon General's Report on Acquired Immune Deficiency Syndrome

FOREWORD

This is a report from the Surgeon General of the U.S. Public Health Service to the public of the United States on AIDS. Acquired Immune Deficiency Syndrome is an epidemic that has already killed thousands of people, mostly young, productive Americans. In addition to illness, disability and death, AIDS has brought fear to the hearts of most Americans—fear of disease and fear of the unknown. Initial reporting of AIDS occurred in the United States, but AIDS and the spread of the AIDS virus is an international problem. This report focuses on prevention that could be applied in all countries.

My report will inform you about AIDS, how it is transmitted, the relative risks of infection and how to prevent it. It will help you understand your fears. Fear can be useful when it helps people avoid behavior that puts them at risk for AIDS. On the other hand, unreasonable fear can be as crippling as the disease itself. If you are participating in activities that could expose you to the AIDS virus, this report could save your life.

In preparing this report I consulted with the best medical and scientific experts this country can offer. I met with leaders of organizations concerned with health, education and other aspects of our society to gain their views of the problems associated with AIDS. The information in this report is current and timely.

This report was written personally by me to provide the necessary understanding of AIDS.

The vast majority of Americans are against illicit drugs. As a health officer I am opposed to the use of illicit drugs. As a practicing physician for more than 40 years, I have seen the devastation that follows the use of illicit drugs—addiction, poor health, family disruption, emotional disturbances and death. I applaud the President's initiative to rid this nation of the curse of illicit drug use and addiction. The success of his initiative is critical to the health of the American people and will also help reduce the number of persons exposed to the AIDS virus.

Some Americans have difficulties in dealing with the subjects of sex, sexual practices and alternate life-styles. Many Americans are opposed to homosexuality, promiscuity of any kind and prostitution.

This report must deal with all of these issues, but does so with the intent that information and education can change individual behavior, since this is the primary way to stop the epidemic of AIDS. This report deals with the positive and negative consequences of activities and behaviors from a health and medical point of view.

Adolescents and pre-adolescents are those whose behavior we wish to especially influence because of their vulnerability when they are exploring their own sexuality (heterosexual and homosexual) and perhaps experimenting with drugs. Teenagers often consider themselves immoral, and these young people may be putting themselves at great risk.

Education about AIDS should start in early elementary school and at home so that children can grow up knowing the behavior to avoid to protect themselves from exposure to the AIDS virus. The threat of AIDS can provide an opportunity for parents to instill in their children their own moral and ethical standards.

Those of us who are parents, educators and community leaders, indeed all adults, cannot disregard this responsibility to educate our young. The need is critical and the price of neglect is high. The lives of our young people depend on our fulfilling our responsibility.

AIDS is an infectious disease. It is contagious, but it cannot be spread in the same manner as a common cold or measles or chicken pox. It is contagious in the same way that sexually transmitted diseases, such as syphilis and gonorrhea, are contagious. AIDS can also be spread through the sharing of intravenous drug needles and syringes used for injecting illicit drugs.

AIDS is *not* spread by common everyday contact but by sexual contact (penis-vagina, penis-rectum, mouth-rectum, mouth-vagina, mouth-penis). Yet there is great misunderstanding resulting in unfounded fear that AIDS can be spread by casual, non-sexual contact. The first cases of AIDS were reported in this country in 1981. We would know by now if AIDS were passed by casual, non-sexual contact.

Today those practicing high risk behavior who become infected with the AIDS virus are found mainly among homosexual and bisexual men and male and female intravenous drug users. Heterosexual transmission is expected to account for an increasing proportion of those who become infected with the AIDS virus in the future.

At the beginning of the AIDS epidemic many Americans had little sympathy for people with AIDS. The feeling was that somehow people from certain groups "deserved" their illness. Let us put those feelings behind us. We are fighting a disease, not people. Those who are already afflicted are sick people and need our care as do all sick patients. The country must face this epidemic as a unified society. We must prevent the spread of AIDS while at the same time preserving our humanity and intimacy.

AIDS is a life-threatening disease and a major public health issue. Its impact on our society is and will continue to be devastating. By the end of 1991, an estimated 270,000 cases of AIDS will have occurred with 179,000 deaths within the decade since the disease was first recognized. In the year 1991, an estimated 145,000 patients with AIDS will need health and supportive services at a total cost of between $8 and $16 billion. However, AIDS is preventable. It can be controlled by changes in personal behavior. It is the responsibility of every citizen to be informed about AIDS and to exercise the appropriate preventive measures. This report will tell you how.

The spread of AIDS can and must be stopped.

C. EVERETT KOOP, M.D., Sc.D.
Surgeon General

AIDS

AIDS Caused by Virus

The letters A-I-D-S stand for Acquired Immune Deficiency Syndrome. When a person is sick with AIDS, he/she is in the final stages of a series of health problems caused by a virus (germ) that can be passed from one person to another chiefly during sexual contact or through the sharing of intravenous drug needles and syringes used for "shooting" drugs. Scientists have named the AIDS virus "HIV or HTLV-III or LAV"*. These abbreviations stand for information denoting a virus that attacks white blood cells (T-Lymphocytes) in the human blood. Throughout this publication we will call the virus the "AIDS virus." The AIDS virus attacks a person's immune system and damages his/her ability to fight other diseases. Without a functioning immune system to ward off other germs, he/she now becomes vulnerable to becoming infected by bacteria, protozoa, fungi and other viruses and malignancies, which may cause life-threatening illness, such as pneumonia, meningitis and cancer.

No Known Cure
There is presently no cure for AIDS. There is presently no vaccine to prevent AIDS.

Virus Invades Blood Stream
When the AIDS virus enters the blood stream, it begins to attack certain white blood cells (T-Lymphocytes). Substances called antibodies are produced by the body. These antibodies can be detected in the blood by a simple test, usually two weeks to three months after infection. Even before the antibody test is positive, the victim can pass the virus to others by methods that will be explained.

Once an individual is infected, there are several possibilities. Some people may remain well but even so they are able to infect others. Others may develop a disease that is less serious than

---

* These are different names given to AIDS virus by the scientific community:

HIV—Human Immunodeficiency Virus.
HTLV-III—Human T-Lymphotropic Virus Type III
LAV—Lymphadenopathy Associated Virus

AIDS referred to as AIDS Related Complex (ARC). In some people the protective immune system may be destroyed by the virus and then other germs (bacteria, protozoa, fungi and other viruses) and cancers that ordinarily would never get a foothold cause "opportunistic diseases"—using the *opportunity* of lowered resistance to infect and destroy. Some of the most common are *Pneumocystis carinii* pneumonia and tuberculosis. Individuals infected with the AIDS virus may also develop certain types of cancers such as Kaposi's sarcoma. These infected people have classic AIDS. Evidence shows that the AIDS virus may also attack the nervous system, causing damage to the brain.

SIGNS AND SYMPTOMS

No Signs
Some people remain apparently well after infection with the AIDS virus. They may have no physically apparent symptoms of illness. However, if proper precautions are not used with sexual contacts and/or intravenous drug use, these infected individuals can spread the virus to others. Anyone who thinks he or she is infected or involved in high risk behaviors should not donate his/her blood, organs, tissues, or sperm because they may now contain the AIDS virus.

ARC
AIDS-Related Complex (ARC) is a condition caused by the AIDS virus in which the patient tests positive for AIDS infection and has a specific set of clinical symptoms. However, ARC patients' symptoms are often less severe than those with the disease we call classic AIDS. Signs and symptoms of ARC may include loss of appetite, weight loss, fever, night sweats, skin rashes, diarrhea, tiredness, lack of resistance to infection, or swollen lymph nodes. These are also signs and symptoms of many other diseases and a physician should be consulted.

AIDS

Only a qualified health professional can diagnose AIDS, which is the result of a natural progress of infection by the AIDS virus. AIDS destroys the body's immune (defense) system and allows otherwise controllable infections to invade the body and cause additional diseases. These opportunistic diseases would not otherwise gain a foothold in the body. These opportunistic diseases may eventually cause death.

Some symptoms and signs of AIDS and the "opportunistic infections" may include a persistent cough and fever associated with shortness of breath or difficult breathing and may be the symptoms of *Pneumocystis carinii* pneumonia. Multiple purplish blotches and bumps on the skin may be a sign of Kaposi's sarcoma. The AIDS virus in all infected people is essentially the same; the reactions of individuals may differ.

Long Term

The AIDS virus may also attack the nervous system and cause delayed damage to the brain. This damage may take years to develop and the symptoms may show up as memory loss, indifference, loss of coordination, partial paralysis or mental disorder. These symptoms may occur alone, or with other symptoms mentioned earlier.

THE PRESENT SITUATION

The number of people estimated to be infected with the AIDS virus in the United States is about 1.5 million. All of these individuals are assumed to be capable of spreading the virus sexually (heterosexually or homosexually) or by sharing needles and syringes or other implements for intravenous drug use. Of these, an estimated 100,000 to 200,000 will come down with AIDS Related Complex (ARC). It is difficult to predict the number who will develop ARC or AIDS because symptoms sometimes take as long as nine years to show up. With our present knowledge, scientists predict that 20 to 30 percent of those infected with the AIDS virus will develop an illness that fits an accepted definition of AIDS within five years. The number of persons known to have AIDS in the United States to date is over 25,000; of these, about half have died of the disease. Since there is no cure, the others are expected to also eventually die from their disease.

The majority of infected antibody positive individuals who carry the AIDS virus show no disease symptoms and may not come down with the disease for many years, if ever.

No Risk from Casual Contact
There is no known risk of non-sexual infection in most of the situations we encounter in our daily lives. We know that family members living with individuals who have the AIDS virus do not become infected except through sexual contact. There is no evidence of transmission (spread) of AIDS virus by everyday contact even though these family members shared food, towels, cups, razors, even toothbrushes, and kissed each other.

Health Workers
We know even more about health care workers exposed to AIDS patients. About 2,500 health workers who were caring for AIDS patients when they were sickest have been carefully studied and tested for infection with the AIDS virus. These doctors, nurses and other health care givers have been exposed to the AIDS patients' blood, stool and other body fluids. Approximately 750 of these health workers reported possible additional exposure by direct contact with a patient's body fluid through spills or being accidentally stuck with a needle. Upon testing these 750, only 3 who had accidentally stuck themselves with a needle had a positive antibody test for exposure to the AIDS virus. Because health workers had much more contact with patients and their body fluids than would be expected from common everyday contact, it

is clear that the AIDS virus is not transmitted by casual contact.

Control of Certain Behaviors Can Stop Further Spread of AIDS
Knowing the facts about AIDS can prevent the spread of the disease. Education of those who risk infecting themselves or infecting other people is the only way we can stop the spread of AIDS. People must be responsible about their sexual behavior and must avoid the use of illicit intravenous drugs and needle sharing. We will describe the types of behavior that lead to infection by the AIDS virus and the personal measures that must be taken for effective protection.

If we are to stop the AIDS epidemic, we all must understand the disease—its cause, its nature, and its prevention. *Precautions must be taken.* The AIDS virus infects persons who expose themselves to known risk behavior, such as certain types of homosexual and heterosexual activities or sharing intravenous drug equipment.

Risks
Although the initial discovery was in the homosexual community, AIDS is not a disease only of homosexuals. AIDS is found in heterosexual people as well. AIDS is not a black or white disease. AIDS is not just a male disease. AIDS is found in women; it is found in children. In the future AIDS will probably increase and spread among people who are not homosexual or intravenous drug abusers in the same manner as other sexually transmitted diseases like syphilis and gonorrhea.

Sex Between Men
Men who have sexual relations with other men are especially at risk. About 70 percent of AIDS victims throughout the country are male homosexuals and bisexuals. This percentage probably will decline as heterosexual transmission increases. *Infection results from a sexual relationship with an infected person.*

Multiple Partners

The risk of infection increases according to the number of sexual partners one has, *male or female.* The more partners you have, the greater the risk of becoming infected with the AIDS virus.

How Exposed

Although the AIDS virus is found in several body fluids, a person acquires the virus during sexual contact with an infected person's blood or semen and possibly vaginal secretions. The virus then enters a person's blood stream through their rectum, vagina or penis.

Small (unseen by the naked eye) tears in the surface lining of the vagina or rectum may occur during insertion of the penis, fingers or other objects, thus opening an avenue for entrance of the virus directly into the blood stream; therefore, the AIDS virus can be passed from penis to rectum and vagina and vice versa without a visible tear in the tissue or the presence of blood.

Prevention of Sexual Transmission—Know Your Partner

Couples who maintain mutually faithful monogamous relationships (only one continuing sexual partner) are protected from AIDS through sexual transmission. If you have been faithful for at least five years and your partner has been faithful too, neither of you is at risk. If you have not been faithful, then you and your partner are at risk. If your partner has not been faithful, then your partner is at risk, which also puts you at risk. This is true for both heterosexual and homosexual couples. Unless it is possible to know with *absolute certainty* that neither you nor your sexual partner is carrying the virus of AIDS, you must use protective behavior.

Absolute certainty means not only that you and your partner have maintained a mutually faithful monogamous sexual relationship, but it means that neither you nor your partner has used illegal intravenous drugs.

YOU CAN PROTECT YOURSELF FROM INFECTION

Some personal measures are adequate to safely protect yourself and others from infection by the AIDS virus and its complications. Among these are:

• If you have been involved in any of the high risk sexual activities described above or have injected illicit intravenous drugs into your body, you should have a blood test to see if you have been infected with the AIDS virus.

• If your test is positive or if you engage in high risk activities and choose not to have a test, you should tell your sexual partner. If you jointly decide to have sex, you must protect your partner by always using a rubber (condom) during (start to finish) sexual intercourse (vagina or rectum).

• If your partner has a positive blood test showing that he/she has been infected with the AIDS virus or you suspect that he/she has been exposed by previous heterosexual or homosexual behavior or use of intravenous drugs with shared needles and syringes, a rubber (condom) should always be used during (start to finish) sexual intercourse (vagina or rectum).

• If you or your partner is at high risk, avoid mouth contact with the penis, vagina or rectum.

• Avoid all sexual activities which could cause cuts or tears in the linings of the rectum, vagina or penis.

• Single teen-age girls have been warned that pregnancy and contracting sexually transmitted diseases can be the result of only one act of sexual intercourse. They have been taught to say *NO* to sex! They have been taught to say *NO* to drugs! By saying *NO* to sex and drugs, they can avoid AIDS which can *kill* them! The same is true for teen-age boys, who should also not have rectal intercourse with other males. It may result in AIDS.

• Do not have sex with prostitutes. Infected male and female prostitutes are frequently also intravenous drug abusers; therefore, they may infect clients by sexual intercourse and other intravenous drug abusers by sharing their intravenous drug equipment. Female prostitutes also can infect their unborn babies.

Intravenous Drug Users

Drug abusers who inject drugs into their veins are another population group at high risk and with high rates of infection by the AIDS virus. Users of intravenous drugs make up 25 percent of the cases of AIDS throughout the country. The AIDS virus is carried in contaminated blood left in the needle, syringe or other drug related implements and the virus is injected into the new victim by reusing dirty syringes and needles. Even the smallest amount of infected blood left in a used needle or syringe can contain live AIDS virus to be passed on to the next user of those dirty implements.

No one should shoot up drugs, because addiction, poor health, family disruption, emotional disturbances and death could follow. However, many drug users are addicted to drugs and for one reason or another have not changed their behavior. For these people, the only way not to get AIDS is *to use a clean, previously unused* needle, syringe or any other implement necessary for the injection of the drug solution.

Hemophilia

Some persons with hemophilia (a blood clotting disorder that makes them subject to bleeding) have been infected with the AIDS virus either through blood transfusion or the use of blood products that help their blood clot. Now that we know how to prepare safe blood products to aid clotting, this is unlikely to happen. This group represents a very small percentage of the cases of AIDS throughout the country.

Blood Transfusion

Currently all blood donors are initially screened and blood is *not* accepted from high risk individuals. Blood that has been collected for use is tested for the presence of antibody to the AIDS virus. However, some people may have had a blood transfusion prior to March, 1985, before we knew how to screen blood for safe transfusion and may have become infected with the AIDS virus. Fortunately there are not now a large number of these cases. With routine testing of blood products, the blood supply for transfusion is now safer than it has ever been with regard to AIDS.

Persons who have engaged in homosexual activities or have "shot" street drugs within the last 10 years should *never* donate blood.

Mother Can Infect Newborn

If a woman is infected with the AIDS virus and becomes pregnant, she is more likely to develop ARC or classic AIDS, and she can pass the AIDS virus to her unborn child.

Approximately one third of the babies born to AIDS-infected mothers will also be infected with the AIDS virus. Most of the infected babies will eventually develop the disease and die. Several of these babies have been born to wives of hemophiliac men infected with the AIDS virus by way of *contaminated* blood products.

Some babies have also been born to women who became infected with the AIDS virus by bisexual partners who had the virus. Almost all babies with AIDS have been born to women who were intravenous drug users or the sexual partners of intravenous drug users who were infected with the AIDS virus. More such babies can be expected.

Think carefully if you plan on becoming pregnant. If there is any chance that you may be in any high risk group or that you have had sex with someone in a high risk group, such as homosexual and bisexual males, drug abusers and their sexual partners, see your doctor.

Summary
AIDS affects certain groups of the population. Homosexual and bisexual males who have had sexual contact with other homosexual or bisexual males as well as those who "shoot" street drugs are at greatest risk of exposure, infection and eventual death. Sexual partners of these high risk individuals are at risk, as well as any children born to women who carry the virus. Heterosexual persons are increasingly at risk.

WHAT IS SAFE

Most Behavior Is Safe
Everyday living does not present any risk of infection. You *cannot* get AIDS from casual social contact. Casual social contact should not be confused with casual *sexual* contact, which is a major cause of the spread of the AIDS virus. Casual *social* contact such as shaking hands, hugging, social kissing, crying, coughing or sneezing, will not transmit the AIDS virus. Nor has AIDS been contracted from swimming in pools or bathing in hot tubs or from eating in restaurants (even if a restaurant worker has AIDS or carries the AIDS virus). AIDS is not contracted from sharing bed linens, towels, cups, straws, dishes or any other eating utensils. You cannot get AIDS from toilets, doorknobs, telephones, office machinery or household furniture. You cannot get AIDS from body massages, masturbation or any non-sexual contact.

Donating Blood
Donating blood is *not* risky at all. *You cannot get AIDS by donating blood.*

Receiving Blood
In the U.S. every blood donor is screened to exclude high risk persons and every blood donation is now tested for the presence

of antibodies to the AIDS virus. Blood that shows exposure to the AIDS virus by the presence of antibodies is not used either for transfusion or for the manufacture of blood products. Blood banks are as safe as current technology can make them. Because antibodies do not form immediately after exposure to the virus, a newly infected person may unknowingly donate blood after becoming infected but before his/her antibody test becomes positive. It is estimated that this might occur less than once in 100,000 donations.

There is no danger of AIDS virus infection from visiting a doctor, dentist, hospital, hairdresser or beautician. AIDS cannot be transmitted non-sexually from an infected person through a health or service provider to another person. Ordinary methods of disinfection for urine, stool and vomitus, which are used for non-infected people are adequate for people who have AIDS or are carrying the AIDS virus. You may have wondered why your dentist wears gloves and perhaps a mask when treating you. This does not mean that he has AIDS or that he thinks you do. He is protecting you and himself from hepatitis, common colds or flu.

There is no danger in visiting a patient with AIDS or caring for him or her. Normal hygienic practices, like wiping of body fluid spills with a solution of water and household bleach (1 part household bleach to 10 parts water), will provide full protection.

Children in School
None of the identified cases of AIDS in the United States are known or are suspected to have been transmitted from one child to another in school, day-care or foster care settings. Transmission would necessitate exposure of open cuts to the blood or other body fluids of the infected child, a highly unlikely occurrence. Even then routine safety procedures for handling blood or other body fluids (which should be standard for all children in the school or day-care setting) would be effective in preventing

transmission from children with AIDS to other children in school. Children with AIDS are highly susceptible to infections, such as chicken pox, from other children. Each child with AIDS should be examined by a doctor before attending school or before returning to school, day-care or foster care settings after an illness. No blanket rules can be made for all school boards to cover all possible cases of children with AIDS and each case should be considered separately and individualized to the child and the setting, as would be done with any child with a special problem, such as cerebral palsy or asthma. A good team to make such decisions with the school board would be the child's parents, physician and a public health official.

Casual social contact between children and persons infected with the AIDS virus is not dangerous.

Insects
There are no known cases of AIDS transmission by insects, such as mosquitoes.

Pets
Dogs, cats and domestic animals are not a source of infection from AIDS virus.

Tears and Saliva
Although the AIDS virus has been found in tears and saliva, no instance of transmission from these body fluids has been reported.

AIDS comes from sexual contacts with infected persons and from the sharing of syringes and needles. There is no danger of infection with AIDS virus by casual social contact.

Testing of Military Personnel
You may wonder why the Department of Defense is currently testing its uniformed services personnel for presence of the AIDS

virus antibody. The military feel this procedure is necessary because the uniformed services act as their own blood bank in a time of national emergency. They also need to protect new recruits (who unknowingly may be AIDS virus carriers) from receiving live virus vaccines. These vaccines could activate disease and be potentially life-threatening to the recruits.

WHAT IS CURRENTLY UNDERSTOOD

Although AIDS is still a mysterious disease in many ways, our scientists have learned a great deal about it. In five years we know more about AIDS than many diseases that we have studied for even longer periods. While there is no vaccine or cure, the results from the health and behavioral research community can only add to our knowledge and increase our understanding of the disease and ways to prevent and treat it.

In spite of all that is known about transmission of the AIDS virus, scientists will learn more. One possibility is the potential discovery of factors that may better explain the mechanism of AIDS infection.

Why are the antibodies produced by the body to fight the AIDS virus not able to destroy that virus?

The antibodies detected in the blood of carriers of the AIDS virus are ineffective, at least when classic AIDS is actually triggered. They cannot check the damage caused by the virus, which is by then present in large numbers in the body. Researchers cannot explain this important observation. We still do not know why the AIDS virus is not destroyed by man's immune system.

SUMMARY

AIDS no longer is the concern of any one segment of society; it is the concern of us all. No American's life is in danger if he/she or their sexual partners do not engage in high risk sexual behavior or use shared needles or syringes to inject illicit drugs into the body. People who engage in high risk sexual behavior or who shoot drugs are risking infection with the AIDS virus and are risking their lives and the lives of others, including their unborn children.

We cannot yet know the full impact of AIDS on our society. From a clinical point of view, there may be new manifestations of AIDS—for example, mental disturbances due to the infection of the brain by the AIDS virus in carriers of the virus. From a social point of view, it may bring to an end the free-wheeling sexual life-style which has been called the sexual revolution. Economically, the care of AIDS patients will put a tremendous strain on our already overburdened and costly health care delivery system.

The most certain way to avoid getting the AIDS virus and to control the AIDS epidemic in the United States is for individuals to avoid promiscuous sexual practices, to maintain mutually faithful monogamous sexual relationships and to avoid injecting illicit drugs.

LOOK TO THE FUTURE

An enormous challenge to public health lies ahead of us and we would do well to take a look at the future. We must be prepared to manage those things we can predict, as well as those we cannot. At the present time there is no vaccine to prevent AIDS. There is no cure. AIDS, which can be transmitted sexually and by sharing needles and syringes among illicit intravenous drug users, is bound to produce profound changes in our society, changes that will affect us all.

Information and Education Only Weapons Against AIDS

It is estimated that in 1991 54,000 people will die from AIDS. At this moment many of them are not infected with the AIDS virus. With proper information and education, as many as 12,000 to

14,000 people could be saved in 1991 from death by AIDS.

AIDS Will Impact All

The changes in our society will be economic and political and will affect our social institutions, our educational practices and our health care. Although AIDS may never touch you personally, the societal impact certainly will.

Be Educated—Be Prepared

Be prepared. Learn as much about AIDS as you can. Learn to separate scientific information from rumor and myth. The Public Health Service, your local public health officials and your family physician will be able to help you.

Concern About Spread of AIDS

While the concentration of AIDS cases is in the larger urban areas today, it has been found in every state and with the mobility of our society, it is likely that cases of AIDS will appear far and wide.

Special Educational Concerns

There are a number of people, primarily adolescents, that do not yet know they will be homosexual or become drug abusers and will not heed this message; there are others who are illiterate and cannot heed this message. They must be reached and taught the risk behaviors that expose them to infection with the AIDS virus.

High Risk Get Blood Test

The greatest public health problem lies in the large number of individuals with a history of high risk behavior who have been infected with and may be spreading the AIDS virus. Those with high risk behavior must be encouraged to protect others by adopting safe sexual practices and by the use of clean equipment for intravenous drug use. If a blood test for antibodies to the AIDS virus is necessary to get these individuals to use safe sexual practices, they should get a blood test. Call your local health department for information on where to get the test.

Anger and Guilt
Some people afflicted with AIDS will feel a sense of anger and others a sense of guilt. In spite of these understandable reactions, everyone must join the effort to control the epidemic, to provide for the care of those with AIDS, and to do all we can to inform and educate others about AIDS, and how to prevent it.

Confidentiality
Because of the stigma that has been associated with AIDS, many afflicted with the disease or who are infected with the AIDS virus are reluctant to be identified with AIDS. Because there is no vaccine to prevent AIDS and no cure, many feel there is nothing to be gained by revealing sexual contacts that might also be infected with the AIDS virus. When a community or a state requires reporting of those infected with the AIDS virus to public health authorities in order to trace sexual and intravenous drug contacts—as is the practice with other sexually transmitted diseases—those infected with the AIDS virus go underground out of the mainstream of health care and education. For this reason current public health practice is to protect the privacy of the individual infected with the AIDS virus and to maintain the strictest confidentiality concerning his/her health records.

State and Local AIDS Task Forces
Many state and local jurisdictions where AIDS has been seen in the greatest numbers have AIDS task forces with heavy representation from the field of public health joined by others who can speak broadly to issues of access to care, provision of care and the availability of community and psychiatric support services.

Such a task force is needed in every community with the power to develop plans and policies, to speak and to act for the good of the public health at every level.

State and local task forces should plan ahead and work collaboratively with other jurisdictions to reduce transmission of AIDS by far-reaching informational and educational programs. As AIDS impacts more strongly on society, they should be charged with making recommendations to provide for the needs of those afflicted with AIDS. They also will be in the best position to answer the concerns and direct the activities of those who are not infected with the AIDS virus.

The responsibility of State and local task forces should be far reaching and might include the following areas:

■ Insure enforcement of public health regulation of such practices as ear piercing and tattooing to prevent transmission of the AIDS virus.

■ Conduct AIDS education programs for police, firemen, correctional institution workers and emergency medical personnel for dealing with AIDS victims and the public.

■ Insure that institutions catering to children or adults who soil themselves or their surroundings with urine, stool and vomitus have adequate equipment for cleanup and disposal, and have policies to insure the practice of good hygiene.

School
Schools will have special problems in the future. In addition to the guidelines already mentioned in this pamphlet, there are other things that should be considered such as sex education and education of the handicapped.

Sex Education
Education concerning AIDS must start at the lowest grade possible as part of any health and hygiene program. The appearance

of AIDS could bring together diverse groups of parents and educators with opposing views on inclusion of sex education in the curricula. There is now no doubt that we need sex education in schools and that it must include information on heterosexual and homosexual relationships. The threat of AIDS should be sufficient to permit a sex education curriculum with a heavy emphasis on prevention of AIDS and other sexually transmitted diseases.

Handicapped and Special Education

Children with AIDS or ARC will be attending school along with others who carry the AIDS virus. Some children will develop brain disease which will produce changes in mental behavior. Because of the right to special education of the handicapped and the mentally retarded, school boards and higher authorities will have to provide guidelines for the management of such children on a case-by-case basis.

Labor and Management

Labor and management can do much to prepare for AIDS so that misinformation is kept to a minimum. Unions should issue preventive health messages because many employees will listen more carefully to a union message than they will to one from public health authorities.

AIDS Education at the Work Site

Offices, factories and other work sites should have a plan in operation for education of the work force and accommodation of AIDS or ARC patients *before* the first such case appears at the work site. Employees with AIDS or ARC should be dealt with as are any workers with a chronic illness. In-house video programs provide an excellent source of education and can be individualized to the needs of a specific work group.

Strain on the Health Care Delivery System

The health care system in many places will be overburdened as it is now in urban areas with large numbers of AIDS patients. It is predicted that during 1991 there will be 145,000 patients requiring hospitalization at least once and 54,000 patients who will die of AIDS. Mental disease (dementia) will occur in some patients who have the AIDS virus before they have any other manifestation such as ARC or classic AIDS.

State and local task forces will have to plan for these patients by utilizing conventional and time honored systems but will also have to investigate alternate methods of treatment and alternate sites for care including homecare.

The strain on the health system can be lessened by family, social and psychological support mechanisms in the community. Programs are needed to train chaplains, clergy, social workers and volunteers to deal with AIDS. Such support is particularly critical to the minority communities.

Mental Health

Our society will also face an additional burden as we better understand the mental health implications of infection by the AIDS virus. Upon being informed of infection with the AIDS virus, a young, active, vigorous person faces anxiety and depression brought on by fears associated with social isolation, illness and dying. Dealing with these individual and family concerns will require the best efforts of mental health professionals.

Controversial Issues

A number of controversial AIDS issues have arisen and will continue to be debated largely because of lack of knowledge about AIDS, how it is spread and how it can be prevented. Among these are the issues of compulsory blood testing, quarantine and identification of AIDS carriers by some visible sign.

Compulsory Blood Testing

Compulsory blood testing of individuals is not necessary. The procedure could be unmanageable and cost prohibitive. It can be expected that many who *test* negatively might actually be positive due to *recent* exposure to the AIDS virus and give a false sense of security to the individual and his/her sexual partners concerning necessary protective behavior. The prevention behavior described in this report, if adopted, will protect the American public and contain the AIDS epidemic. Voluntary testing will be available to those who have been involved in high risk behavior.

Quarantine

Quarantine has no role in the management of AIDS because AIDS is not spread by casual contact. The only time that some form of quarantine might be indicated is in a situation where an individual carrying the AIDS virus knowingly and willingly continues to expose others through sexual contact or sharing drug equipment. Such circumstances should be managed on a case-by-case basis by local authorities.

Identification of AIDS Carriers by Some Visible Sign

Those who suggest the marking of carriers of the AIDS virus by some visible sign have not thought the matter through thoroughly. It would require testing of the entire population, which is unnecessary, unmanageable and costly. It would miss those recently infected individuals who would test negatively, but be infected. The entire procedure would give a false sense of security. AIDS must and will be treated as a disease that can infect anyone. AIDS should not be used as an excuse to discriminate against any group or individual.

Updating Information

As the Surgeon General, I will continually monitor the most current and active health, medical and scientific information and make it available to you, the American people. Armed with this information you can join in the discussion and resolution of AIDS-related issues that are critical to your health, your children's health and the health of the nation.

Information Sources
U.S. Public Health Service
Public Affairs Office
Hubert H. Humphrey Bldg.
Room 725-H
200 Independence Ave., S.W.
Washington, D.C. 20201
(202) 245-6867

Local Red Cross or American Red Cross AIDS Education Offic
1730 D St., N.W.
Washington, D.C. 20006
(202) 737-8300

Book List

The books listed here may provide additional help for you and members of your Bible study group on the topics discussed in this course. Gospel Light does not necessarily endorse the entire contents of all publications referred to in this list.

Intoxicants

Gehring, W. Robert, M.D. *Rx for Addiction.* Grand Rapids: Zondervan, 1985.

Strack, Jay. *Drugs and Drinking: The All American Cop-Out.* Nashville: Thomas Nelson, 1979.

Alcoholism

Dunn, Jerry G. *God Is for the Alcoholic.* Chicago: Moody Press, 1967.

Wilkerson, David. *Sipping Saints.* Old Tappan: Fleming H. Revell Company, 1979.

Coping with Trauma in the Home
Augsburger, David. *Caring Enough to Confront: The Love-Fight.* Ventura: Regal Books, 1974.
Sehnert, Keith W., M.D. *Stress/Unstress.* Minneapolis: Augsburg Publishing House, 1981.
Timmons, Tim. *Stress in the Family: How to Live Through It.* Eugene: Harvest House Publications, 1982.

Incest
Foward, Susan and Buck, Craig. *Betrayal of Innocence: Incest and Its Devastation.* New York: Penguin Books, 1978.
Janssen, Martha. *Silent Scream.* Philadelphia: Fortress Press, 1983.
Peters, David. *A Betrayal of Innocence.* Waco: Word Books, 1986.

Physical Abuse
Finkelhor, David. *A Sourcebook on Child Sexual Abuse.* Beverly Hills: Sage Publications, 1986.
Olson, Esther L. and Petersen, Kenneth. *No Place to Hide.* Wheaton: Tyndale Publishing House, 1982.

Homosexuality
Baker, Don. *Beyond Rejection: The Church, Homosexuality and Hope.* Oregon: Multnomah Press, 1985.

AIDS
Antonio, Gene. *The AIDS Cover-up? The Real and Alarming Facts About AIDS.* San Francisco: Ignatius Press, 1986.
McKeever, Dr. James. *The AIDS Plague.* Medford: Omega Publications, 1986.
Redfield, M.D. and Franz, Wanda. *AIDS and Young People. Washington, D.C.: Regency Publishers, 1987.*

Bigotry/Interracial Relationships

Perkins, John M. *Let Justice Roll Down.* Ventura: Regal Books, 1976.

Rausch, David A. *A Legacy of Hatred: Why Christians Must Not Forget the Holocaust.* Chicago: Moody Press, 1985.

Ten Boom, Corrie and Sherrill, John. *The Hiding Place.* Old Tappan: Fleming H. Revell Company, 1974.

Tutu, Desmond. *Hope and Suffering: Sermons and Speeches.* Grand Rapids: William B. Eerdmans Publishing Company, 1984.

New Age

Groothuis, Douglas R. *Unmasking the New Age.* Downers Grove: InterVarsity Press, 1986.

————. *Confronting the New Age.* Downers Grove: InterVarsity Press, 1988.

Hexham, Irving and Poewe, Karla. *Understanding Cults and New Religions.* Grand Rapids: Eerdmans, 1986.

Hoyt, Karen, ed. *The New Age Rage.* Old Tappan: Fleming H. Revell, 1987.

Sire, James W. *The Universe Next Door.* 2nd ed. Downers Grove: InterVarsity Press, 1988.

Walsh, Brian J. and Middleton, J. Richard. *The Transforming Vision.* Downers Grove, InterVarsity Press, 1984.

Sanctity of Life

Allen, Ronald B. *The Majesty of Man: The Dignity of Being Human.* Portland: Multnomah Press, 1984.

Baker, Don. *Beyond Choice: The Abortion Story No One Is Telling.* Portland: Multnomah Press, 1985.

Koop, C. Everett. *The Right to Live, the Right to Die.* Wheaton: Tyndale House Publishers, 1980.

Koop, C. Everett and Schaeffer, Francis A. *Whatever Happened to the Human Race?* Westchester: Crossway Books, 1983.

Powell, John. *Abortion: The Silent Holocaust.* Valencia: Tabor

Publishing, 1981.

President Ronald W. Reagan: *Abortion and the Conscience of the Nation*. Washington, D.C.: Government Printing Office, 1983.

Whitehead, John W., ed. *Arresting Abortion: Practical Ways to Save Unborn Children*. Westchester: Crossway Books, 1985.

Aging

Becker, Arthur H. *Ministry with Older Persons: A Guide for Clergy and Congregations*. Minneapolis: Augsburg Publishing House, 1986.

War and Violence

Amstutz, Mark R. *Christian Ethics and U.S. Foreign Policy*. Grand Rapids: Zondervan Publishing House, 1987.

Clouse, Robert G. *War: Four Christian Views*. Downers Grove: InterVarsity Press, 1985.

Graham, Daniel O. *High Frontier: A Strategy for National Survival*. New York: Pinnacle Books, 1983.

McSorley, Richard. *New Testament Basis of Peacemaking*. Scottdale: Herald Press, 1985.

Morey, Robert A. *When Is It Right to Fight?* Minneapolis: Bethany House Publishers, 1985.

Sterba, James P. *Morality in Practice*. 2nd ed. Belmont: Wadsworth Publishing Co., 1988.

Walzer, Michael. *Just and Unjust Wars*. New York: Basic Books, 1977.

Yoder, John H. *He Came Preaching Peace*. Scottdale: Herald Press, 1985.

Sexual Roles in Our Culture

Blitchington, W. Peter. *Sex Roles and the Christian Family*. Wheaton: Tyndale House Publishers, 1984.

Blitchington, W. Peter and Evelyn. *Understanding the Male Ego*. Nashville: Thomas Nelson Publishers, 1984.

Elliot, Elisabeth. *The Mark of a Man*. Old Tappan: Fleming H.

Revell, 1981.

Getz, Gene A. *The Measure of a Man*. Ventura: Regal Books, 1974.

Divorce

Duty, Guy. *Divorce and Remarriage*. Minneapolis: Bethany House Publishers, 1967.

Smoke, Jim. *Living Beyond Divorce*. Eugene: Harvest House Publishers, 1984.

————. *Growing Through Divorce*. Eugene: Harvest House Publishers, 1984.

Sex

Alcorn, Andy. *Christians in the Wake of the Sexual Revolution: Rediscovering Our Sexual Sanity*. Portland: Multnomah Press, 1985.

Burns, Jim. *Handling Your Hormones*. Laguna Hills: Merit Books, 1984.

Dobson, James. *Preparing for Adolescence*. Ventura: Vision House, 1984.

Leman, Kevin. *Smart Girls Don't; and Guys Don't Either*. Ventura: Regal Books, 1982.

Women in the Church

Malcolm, Dari Torgesen. *Women at the Crossroads*. Downers Grove: InterVarsity Press, 1982.

General

Birch, Bruce C. and Rasmussen, Larry. *Bible and Ethics in the Christian Life*. Minneapolis: Augsburg Publishing House, 1976.

Chambers, Oswald. *Biblical Ethics*. Fort Washington: Christian Literature Crusade, 1964.

Smedes, Lewis B. *Mere Morality: What God Expects from Ordinary People*. Grand Rapids: William B. Eerdmans, 1983.

Meet the Authors

Judy Alexandre is the director of a counseling center and a diplomate in clinical social work. She is a frequent seminar and conference speaker. One of her counseling specialties is working with individuals recovering from childhood trauma. Judy has her Ph.D. in Social Psychology.

Ruth M. Bathauer is an editor, an author and is product and proofreading manager for Regal Books. She is also a professional member of the National Writers Club and the National League of Pen Women. Ruth's most recent book is entitled *Parent Care: A Guide to Help Adult Children Provide Care and Support for Their Aging Parents.*

Rick Bundschuh is a nationally known youth worker and author. He is a frequent speaker at camps, seminars and churches across the country. Rick is currently associate pastor of Kalaheo Missionary Church in Kauai, Hawaii.

David Edwards is currently a computer programmer and a free-lance songwriter. Besides writing for Gospel Light, he has also written for Campus Life. With the David Edwards Band, he recorded two albums with Word and one album with Lexicon. David and his family live in upstate New York.

Charles Mylander is general superintendent of the Friends Church Southwest Yearly Meeting and is also adjunct professor at Azusa Pacific University's Graduate School of Theology. He is a frequent guest speaker at churches, conferences and retreats. His speaking emphasizes practical Christian living.

Annette Parrish is an award-winning writer and has served as a managing editor for Gospel Light. She has also served as a children's minister, a representative to a Christian lobby in Washington, D.C. and as a member of a denominational Board of Christian Social Concerns and Board of Christian Education.

Eric Pement is associate editor for *Cornerstone* magazine in Chicago. He is also the executive director for Evangelical Ministries to New Religions.

John M. Perkins is founder and president of the John Perkins Foundation for Reconciliation and Development and the founder and president emeritus of the Voice of Calvary Ministry. His books include *Let Justice Roll Down* and *With Justice for All. John Perkins: Land Where My Father Died*, written by Gordon D. Aeschliman, is a book of insight into the heart and mind of John Perkins.

Jim Reeves has a private practice with the Chemical Dependency Program in Lakewood, Colorado. He lives in Arvada, Colorado.

Tracy L. Scott has her M.A. in Theology from Fuller Theological Seminary. She has worked as a research and teaching assistant for Dr. Richard Mouw in such classes as Christian World View and Contemporary Challenge, and Social Ethics. She is pursuing a Ph.D. in Sociology of Religion at Princeton and is hoping to teach sociology at the college level.

Jon Trott is an editor and writer for *Cornerstone* magazine. He has been a lyricist for REZ Band and has written for *Eternity* and *CCM*. Jon is currently pursuing a book on satanism and one on political action in the American housing crisis from a

ristian perspective. He received the 1989 reporting award from
Evangelical Press Association.

Don Williams is currently the pastor of Coast Vineyard in
an Diego, California. He was on the staff of The First Presbyte-
rian Church of Hollywood for 10 years and has taught at Fuller
Theological Seminary. Don has his M.Div. from Princeton Seminary and his Ph.D. from Columbia University. Among his writings
are *The Apostle Paul and Women in the Church* and, most recently, *Signs, Wonders and the Kingdom of God.*

Notes